CLASSIC SONGS OF THE 40s

Project Managers: Tony Esposito & Carol Cuellar

Text By: Fucini Productions, Inc.

Cover Design: Joseph Klucar

Art Layout: Martha L. Ramirez

Production Coordinator: Donna Salzburg

Contents

Introduction

The 1940s . . . Has there ever been a time when ordinary people have met so many extraordinary challenges with such splendid courage? In this eventful ten-year period, Americans overcame the lingering depravations of the Great Depression, defeated the totalitarian forces of Nazism and Fascism in World War II, and confronted the Soviet Union in a Cold War stand-off of atomic super-powers.

Obviously, the great events of the decade demanded bold actions and unselfish sacrifice. Americans from all walks of life responded to this challenge with energy, optimism, and unfailing courage.

There were heroes everywhere in the '40s: "Rosie the Riveter," who stepped onto the factory floor when her husband and brother went off to war so that the nation's industrial machine could continue to turn out the tanks and airplanes needed to defeat Hitler's armies; civil rights leaders whose eloquent words compelled America to start living up to her constitution's promise of equality for all; and the young soldiers and sailors who sacrificed their lives in faraway places so the dreams of others could one day come true.

Music helped sustain members of America's "Greatest Generation" through the frightening and uncertain times of the '40s. Events around the world may have been unfolding at a dizzying pace, but everyone could take comfort in listening to a familiar star like Bing Crosby sing "I'll Remember April." Sure, the war had separated lovers, but you could always soothe a lonely heart with romantic songs like Glenn Miller's "Fools Rush In," Ella Fitzgerald's "How High the Moon," or Patti Page's "So in Love."

The grim realities of the '40s never robbed Americans of their sense of humor. People who had learned that a good chuckle was a great tonic for the hard economic times of the '30s continued to rely on the magic of laughter to help them through the frightening challenges of the new decade. Funny songs like "Cement Mixer (Put-ti, Put-ti)," "Five Guys Named Moe," and Betty Hutton's "Pistol Packin' Mama" helped lift the country's spirits during the tumultuous, and often frightening, '40s.

Good music was never very far from anyone during this fast-paced decade, thanks to the growth of radio and the popularity of a recent innovation called the jukebox. Big and colorful, brightly lighted jukeboxes were a common sight at taverns, restaurants, diners, lodges, and even gas stations. Put a nickel in, and you could hear the latest hit from Frank Sinatra, Benny Goodman, or any of the '40s stars. A quarter would entitle you to six selections.

So go ahead and enjoy this jukebox collection of songs from the '40s. You don't even need to drop a coin down the slot. Just let your ears and your imagination transport you back to the music that moved America during one of the country's greatest decades.

Music Goes to War

The United States entered World War II on December 7, 1941, following the Japanese air raid on Pearl Harbor. Brushing aside their shock and setting aside their differences after the attack, Americans rolled up their sleeves and came together to work toward the defeat of the nation's enemies.

Like Americans from all walks of life, musicians and recording artists did their part to contribute to the war effort. Some joined the armed services and saw action on the front line. Others helped bolster the morale of troops by bringing the sweet sounds of home to distant battlefields in USO shows.

Among the most tireless entertainers of American troops were the Andrews Sisters. LaVerne, Maxene, and Patty Andrews were a whirlwind of musical energy. During the course of their career, the Andrews Sisters recorded more than 1,800 songs and sold more than 90 million records. Their recording of "Boogie Woogie Bugle Boy" was one of the most popular songs of the '40s. The singing sisters' cheerful optimism resonated with audiences during the war years, when Americans in and out of the military were determined to keep their spirits high.

The Andrews Sisters often performed with Glenn Miller on tours of military bases. America's most popular band leader, Miller joined the Army shortly after America entered the war and was commissioned a captain.

Assigned to the Army Air Corps (the predecessor of the Air Force), Miller organized a band to entertain fighting troops. The Glenn Miller Army Air Force Band criss-crossed the battlefront, performing more than 800 live concerts during the war, more than half of which were broadcast on radio.

For American soldiers on the front, a visit from Miller and his band was about as welcome as a letter and a photograph from a loved one back home. It didn't matter where you were from, what color your skin was, or what rung on the economic ladder you occupied, if you came of age in the late '30s or early '40s, you knew and loved Miller's graceful blend of swing, jazz, and improvisation.

Miller recorded many phenomenal hits in the years leading up to the war. Perhaps the most memorable of them, and the one most often associated with his band by troops, was "Chattanooga Choo Choo." Recorded in 1941 for the film *Sun Valley Serenade,* the song's playful lyrics and perky melody offered an upbeat flight of fancy that brightened the hearts of soldiers and civilians during the dark war years.

However, something more was at work behind the popularity of "Chattanooga Choo Choo." Taking us from Pennsylvania Station in New York on through Baltimore and the Deep South until we arrived in Tennessee, the song tapped into a feeling of war-time patriotism by reminding people that, despite its regional differences, America was one nation.

Like "Chattanooga Choo Choo," many of Miller's most popular songs revolved around place themes. Listening to songs like "Along the Santa Fe Trail" and "I've Got a Gal in Kalamazoo" evoked images of home for lonely soldiers.

On December 15, 1944, Miller was flying from England to France when his military plane went down over the water. Repeated searches failed to turn up any trace of Miller's aircraft. Ironically, the gifted band leader whose music had provided so many soldiers with an emotional connection to life back in America would never have a homecoming of his own.

Bebop Generation

Jazz both celebrated and reflected the diversity of American society during the '40s in much the same way that it did in the previous decade. On one level, this dynamic American music genre continued the big-band sound, with Duke Ellington and other artists treating us to sophisticated orchestral works like "Don't Get Around Much Anymore." Meanwhile, another group of younger musicians took the smaller club sound of the '30s and developed it into a new form of jazz expression that became known as *bebop* (later shortened to *bop*).

Led by the brilliant saxophonist from Kansas City, Charlie "Yardbird" Parker, young bebop musicians blazed a new path, creating a sound that would resonate in jazz for the rest of the twentieth century and beyond—first as "cool jazz," then as "funk" and "fusion." Bebop fans packed clubs in New York, Chicago, and other cities to savor the intricate melodies and dazzling solo improvisations of the new generation of bebop artists.

Bebop conveyed a sense of both complexity and urgency, as evidenced in Parker songs like "Laura." This made it an ideal form of music for the '40s, a decade that saw profound changes (like the dawn of the atomic age) reshape society in what felt like the blink of an eye.

The musicians who performed bebop were talented artists with extraordinary techniques. They played long resplendent phrases with multiple notes and took innovative turns in melodic directions. An element of surprise was essential to their performances. For example, there would be a sudden break in a song, a bass drum would add a surprise accent, or a pianist might insert elaborate and unexpected chords to a piece at irregular intervals.

A key figure in the development of bebop was Billy Eckstine ("Taking a Chance on Love"). Eckstine was a singer with the popular Earl Hines band in the early '40s. It was at the urging of Eckstine that Hines hired the rising young genius Charlie Parker, lending added force to bebop. Eckstine formed his own band, which showcased bebop artists like Parker and the hot young trumpet player Miles Davis. Eckstine initially hired the teenage Davis as a temporary replacement for a horn player who had taken ill.

As a young man in the mid-'40s, Davis roomed with Parker in New York, studying and absorbing the great saxophonist's insights. Later in the decade, Davis took bebop to the next level by pioneering the "cool jazz" sound. Taking the fast-running-style chords of bebop, Davis developed a more modal sound, changing chords every other measure.

In songs like "'Round Midnight," he demonstrated the soft and rich tones, sensitive pauses, and relaxed, almost delayed, beat that were to define the "cool" sound of the next generation and become his personal trademark. Just as his hero Parker had in the early '40s, Davis ended the decade pushing jazz to new limits.

Jukebox Saturday Night

Jukeboxes, with their brightly colored lights and shiny metal frames, became one of the most enduring symbols of America in the '40s. Although organ maker Farny Wurlitzer first began selling his coin-operated record-playing machines in the 1930s, the jukebox didn't hit its stride until the '40s, when the compact 45 rpm record appeared.

Soon, jukeboxes were everywhere, from the corner tavern and neighborhood candy store to the fancy restaurant downtown. The proliferation of these big, gaudy machines made hit recordings accessible to everybody. You didn't need to own a record player; just drop a coin down the slot, and the latest song from Judy Garland or Frank Sinatra was yours to enjoy.

Jukeboxes turned any establishment, even the humblest diner, into a swinging dance floor. When it came to jukebox dances, one of the most popular artists was band leader and trumpet player Harry James. As he demonstrated again and again in songs like "I Had the Craziest Dream,"

James had an uncanny ability to get his band to swing at the right tempo on everything from beautiful ballads to hot jazz tunes.

James' band showcased many of the singers who would become jukebox stars. Dick Haymes, the vocalist for James in the early '40s, possessed one of the best romantic baritones of the era and earned nine gold records during the decade. Haymes swept fans off of their feet with a string of hits, including "Five Minutes More," "The More I See You," and "You Make Me Feel So Young."

Frank Sinatra was discovered by James and performed as his vocalist for a year before joining the Tommy Dorsey band. Sinatra's smooth vocals were jukebox favorites that spoke to the longings and aspirations of young Americans in songs like "Almost Like Being in Love" and "You'll Never Know."

Another jukebox legend was "Swing and Sway" Sammy Kaye, the band leader whose lilting rhythm styles made him a favorite of dancers. Singer, guitarist, and composer Eddy Howard's sweet tunes like "Put 'Em in a Box, Tie 'Em With a Ribbon" were also popular jukebox selections.

So even though commodities like sugar and gasoline were rationed during the lean war years of the '40s, there was never a shortage of good music, thanks to the creative genius of our jukebox legends.

Rushing Into a New World

The '40s were a time of profound change, a decade when the future seemed to introduce itself. Many of the events and developments that would define the twentieth century happened in the '40s. World War II, the Cold War, and the introduction of atomic weapons, all of which reshaped the world's political landscape, came about in this pivotal decade. The computer, jet airplane, commercial television, and other innovations developed in the '40s are still affecting daily life in new ways today.

As it did in other areas of life, the '40s brought changes to the world of music that reverberated throughout the rest of the century. The doo-wop style of singing that lent such a powerful impetus to rock 'n' roll in the '50s can be traced back to the '40s, when artists like the Ink Spots pioneered the group-harmony genre of singing.

In their smash hits of the '40s like "I Don't Want to Set the World on Fire," the Ink Spots introduced popular music fans to a new vocal style that emphasize harmony, a clear tenor vibrato, and understated but elegant accompaniments. Bill Kenny, the group's lead singer, was known for his perfect diction and fluttering vocals, which played off beautifully against the deep drawl of singing partner Hoppy Jones' rich bass. The perfect harmonies of Carlie Fuqua and Deek Watson rounded out the sensational Ink Spots sound, paving the way for a generation of singers to come.

While the Ink Spots were developing a new style that would bring street-corner harmonizing to the forefront of popular music, other artists like Stan Kenton and Lionel Hampton were experimenting with innovations that would move big-band jazz from the dance hall to the concert hall.

After playing for big bands, Kenton formed The Stan Kenton Orchestra in 1941. The jazz group was eventually re-named after Kenton's wildly popular theme song "Artistry in Rhythm." Always eager to experiment with new ideas, Kenton pioneered the concept of odd-meter jazz, giving his music a more airy orchestral sound.

Around the same time that Kenton was forming his orchestra, world-renowned vibraphonist Lionel Hampton started his namesake band after years of playing with Benny Goodman. Hampton gave the vibraphone an identity in jazz, applying the instrument to swing pieces in ways that no one had ever imagined possible. In songs like “Hey! Ba-Ba-Re-Bop,” he created his famous vibe riffs that would be loved by fans throughout the world.

As the leader of his own band, Hampton explored different forms of musical expression, creating a more complex ensemble sound to go along with his swing pieces. In later years, he applied his genius to symphonic compositions in works like “King David Suite” and “Blues Suite,” which have been performed by many of the world’s leading orchestras. In keeping with the adventuresome spirit of American music of the ’40s, the gifted vibraphonist and composer from Louisville, Kentucky, left a legacy of creative innovation that will always be treasured.

Things That First Appeared in the ’40s

1. Velcro
2. Digital computers
3. Jet aircraft
4. The Tony Awards
5. 45 rpm records
6. Commercial television networks
7. Automatic bowling pin spotters
8. Baskin-Robbins ice cream
9. Ferrari automobiles
10. Tupperware food containers
11. Solid-state transistors
12. Electro-photocopying machines (Xerox)

TAKING A CHANCE ON LOVE

Words by
JOHN LATOUCHE and TED FETTER

Music by
VERNON DUKE

Cmaj7
Edim
Dm7
G7
C
C+
Chorus, Moderately
mp
Here I go a - gain I hear those trum-pets blow a - gain
Here I come a - gain I'm gon - na make things hum a - gain
Here I slip a - gain a - bout to take that tip a - gain
Am
Am7
D7
Dm7
G7
Em7
Cm
all a - glow a - gain Tak - ing A Chance On Love
act - ing dumb a - gain Tak - ing A Chance On Love
got my grip a - gain Tak - ing A Chance On Love
Here I slide a - gain a - bout to take that ride a - gain
Here I stand a - gain a - bout to beat the band a - gain
Now I prove a - gain that I can make life move a - gain
star - ry - eyed a - gain Tak - ing A Chance On Love. I
feel - ing grand a - gain Tak - ing A Chance On Love. I
in the groove a - gain Tak - ing A Chance On Love I

Gm7 C7 F Cdim Gm7 Gdim F
thought that cards — were a frame - up — I nev - er — would try But
nev - er dreamed in my slum - bers — and bets were — ta - boo But
walk a - round — with a horse - shoe — in clo - ver — I lie And
mf
Fm7 Bb7 Eb Gdim Fm7 Ab7 G7+
now I'm tak - ing the game up — and the ace of hearts is high
now I'm play - ing the num - bers on a lit - tle dream for two
broth - er rab - bit of course you — bet - ter kiss your foot good - bye
C Edim Dm7 G7 C C+
Things are mend - ing now — I see a rain - bow blend - ing now —
Wad - ing in a - gain — I'm lead - in' with my chin a - gain —
On the ball a - gain — I'm rid - in' for a fall a - gain —
sfz mp
Am Am7 D7 Dm7 G7 C Dm7 G7 C
1. 2.
we'll have our hap - py end - ing now Tak - ing A Chance On Love.
I'm start - in' out to win a - gain Tak - ing A Chance On Love.
I'm gon - na give my all a - gain Tak - ing A Chance On Love. —
f
3
sfz

ALONG THE SANTA FE TRAIL

Words by
AL DUBIN and EDWINA COOLIDGE

Music by
WILL GROSZ

Ebm
Bbaug
Ebm
Db7aug
You are the pic-ture and they on-ly form the frame for since you came, the des-ert
Gb
E7
Bbaug
Ebm
Bb7
Ebm
Eb
Bb7
does-n't seem the same; And at the end of each day:
REFRAIN
(Sweetly)
Eb
Bbaug
Eb
F9
An - gels come to paint the des-ert night - ly When the moon is beam-ing
p-f
Ab6
Abm6
Ab6
Eb
Bbaug
bright - ly A-LONG THE SAN-TA FE TRAIL.

Eb
Bbaug
Eb
Bbaug
F9
Star - dust scat-tered all a - long the high - way
Ab6
Abm6
Ab6
On a rain-bow col-ored sky - way A-LONG THE SAN-TA FE
Eb
Bbm7
Eb7
Ab
TRAIL. Be - side you I'm rid - ing
Abm6
Eb
ev - 'ry hill and dale while shad - ows hide you

F7
Abm6
Bbaug
just like a pret-ty pur-ple veil; There-by hangs a tale, I
Eb
Bbaug
Eb
Bbaug
F9
found you and the moun-tains that sur - round you
Ab6
Abm6
Ab6
are the walls I built a - round you A-LONG THE SAN-TA FE
1. Eb
Abmaj7
Bb9
2. Eb
TRAIL.
TRAIL.

BOOGIE WOOGIE BUGLE BOY

Words and Music by
DON RAYE and HUGHIE PRINCE

C6

but then his num - ber came up___ and he was gone with the draft._ He's in the

G7 F9 C6

ar - my now a blow - in' re - veil - le. He's the Boo - gie Woo - gie Bu - gle Boy of

C6

Com - pa - ny B.___ They made him blow a bu - gle for his Un - cle Sam;__ it

. . . end solo) He puts the boys to sleep with boo - gie ev - 'ry night,_ and

real - ly brought him down be - cause he could not jam.___ The cap - tain

wakes them up the same way in the ear - ly bright.__ They clap their

F9
C6
seemed to un - der - stand,
hands and stamp their feet,
be - cause the next day the "cap" went out and
be - cause they know how he plays when some - one
G7
3
draft - ed a band. And now the com - pa - ny jumps
gives him a beat. He real - ly breaks them up
when he plays
F9
C6
re - veil - le. He's the Boo - gie Woo - gie Bu - gle Boy of Com - pa - ny B. A
C6
3
root, a toot, a toot - di - dle ah - da toot. He blows eight to the bar
3

F9
in boo - gie rhy - thm. He can't blow a note un - less a bass and gui - tar is play - in'
C6
with him.
G7
3
And the com - pa - ny jumps when he plays
F9
To Coda
C6
re - veil - le. He's the Boo - gie Woo - gie Bu - gle Boy of Com - pa - ny B.
N.C.
He was some Boo - gie Woo - gie Bu - gle Boy of Com - pa - ny B.

F9
When he played boo - gie woo - gie bu - gle, he was
C6
bus - y as a bus - y bee.
And when he played, he made the com-pa-ny jump
G7
3
F9
eight to the bar. He's the Boo - gie Woo - gie Bu - gle Boy of Com-pa - ny B. Ah - da
C6
C6
3
3
toot did-dle ah - da toot did-dle ah - da toot - toot. He goes eight to the bar.

F9
He can't blow a note if a bass ___ and gui - tar ___ is - n't
C6
with him. ___
G7
3
And ___ the com-pa-ny jumps when he plays
F9
C6
D.S. 𝄋 al Coda
re - veil - le. He's the Boo - gie Woo - gie Bu - gle Boy of Com - pa - ny B. ___

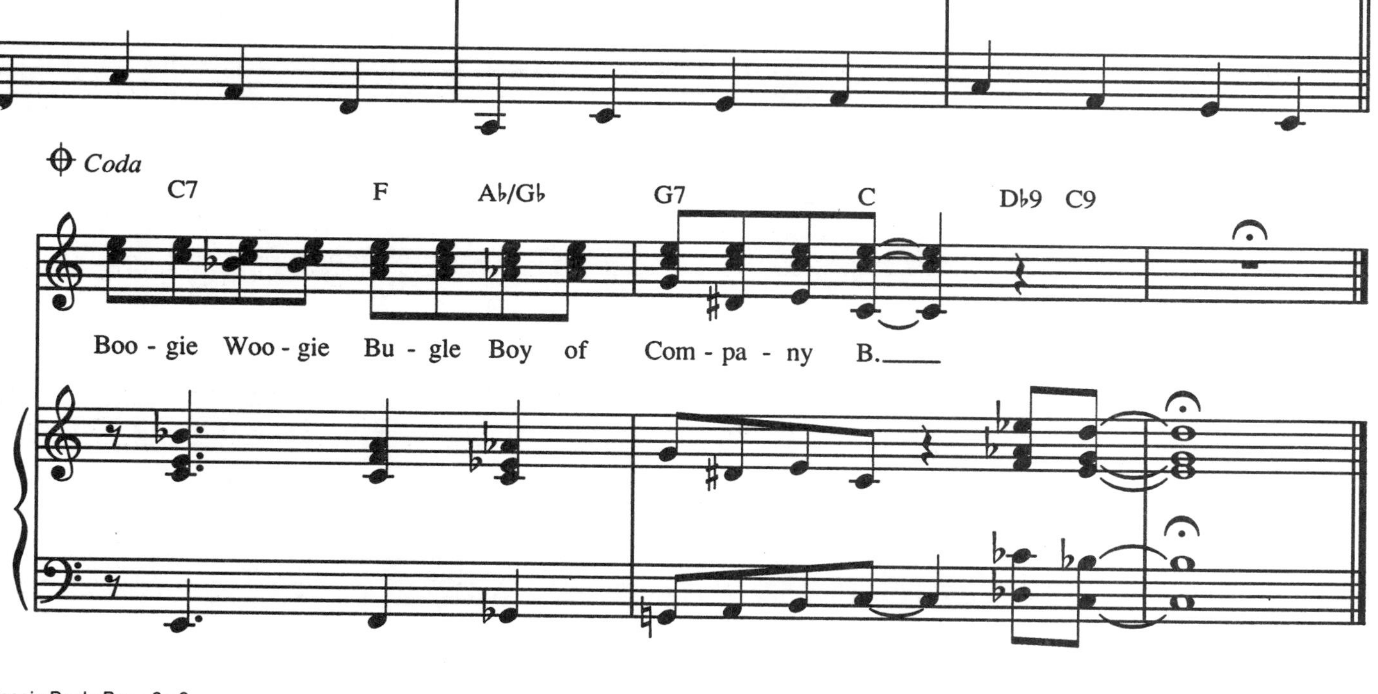
𝄌 Coda
C7
F
A♭/G♭
G7
C
D♭9 C9
Boo - gie Woo - gie Bu - gle Boy of Com - pa - ny B. ___

I COULD WRITE A BOOK

Words by
LORENZ HART

Music by
RICHARD RODGERS

Gm7
But my bus - y mind is burn - ing to
C7
Fmaj7
use what learn - ing I've got,
Em7
A7
D7
I won't waste an - y time,
G
I'll
G7
strike while the
Dm7
i - ron is
G7
hot.
Refrain (slowly, with expression)
C
If they asked me
G7
I could write a
C
book,
p
G7
— A - bout the
C
way you
G7
walk and
C
whis - per
C♯dim
and

Dm7
G7
F
G7
C
A♭7
Dm7
G7
look, I could write a pre - face on
più espress.
C
F♯ dim
G
C
F♯dim
G
E♭7
Am7
D7
how we met, so the world would nev - er for -
G
Dm7
G7
C
G7
get, And the sim - ple se - cret of the
mf
p
C
G7
C
G7
plot is just to tell them that I

C
C♯dim
Dm7
G7
F
G7
love you a lot, Then the
più espress.
C
A♭7
Dm7
G7
Gm7
C7
world dis - cov - ers as my book
F
Dm
C
C+
Dm7
G7
ends, How to make two lov - ers of
1.
C
Dm7
G7
2.
C
F
C
friends. If they friends.
mf
mf

BEAT ME DADDY, EIGHT TO THE BAR

Words and Music by
DON RAYE, HUGHIE PRINCE and ELEANOR SHEEHY

B♭
B♭7
Bdim7
but the style he likes the best is eight to the bar.
F7
When he plays it's a ball, he's the dad - dy of them
B♭
E♭6
B♭
B♭
all.
The peo - ple gath - er a - round when he
B♭7
gets on the stand, then when he plays he gets a hand. The

E♭
3 fr
B♭
rhy - thm he beats puts the cats in a trance, no - bod - y there
F7
both - ers to dance. But when he jams with the bass and gui - tar,
B♭
C♯dim7
Cm7
3 fr
F7
B♭
they hol - ler, "Aw, beat me, dad - dy, eight to the bar." A
plink, a plank, a plink plank plink plank plunk - in' on the keys,

B♭7
E♭
3fr
a riff, a raff, a riff raff riff raff
B♭
riff - in' out with ease.
And when he
F7
jams with the bass and gui - tar,
they hol - ler, "Aw,
B♭
C♯dim7
1
Cm7
F7
B♭
2
Cm7
F7
B♭
beat me, dad - dy, eight to the bar." The peo - ple eight to the bar."

HOW HIGH THE MOON

Words by
NANCY HAMILTON

Music by
MORGAN LEWIS

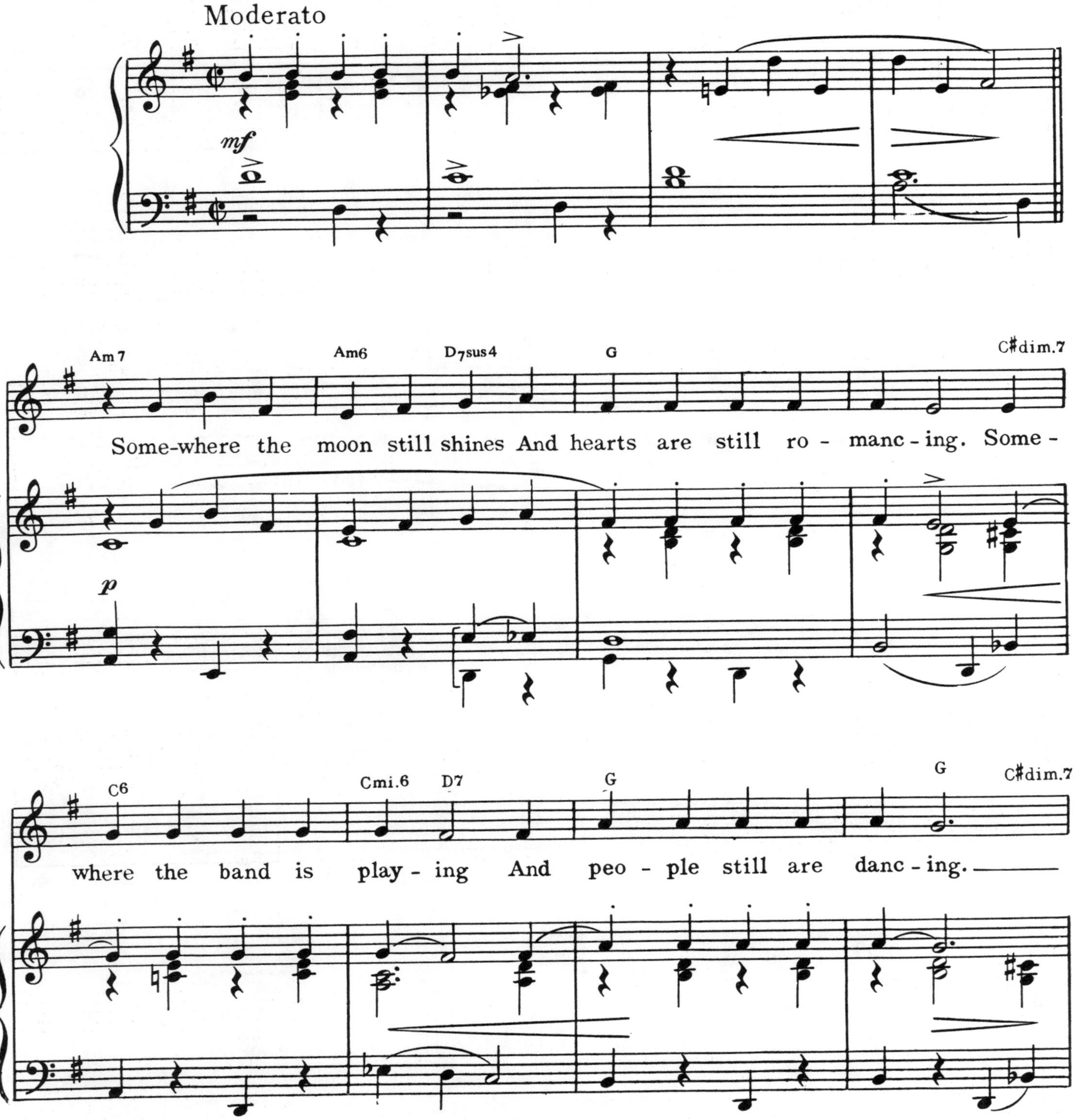

Am7 Am6 D7sus4 G C#dim.7

Some-where the moon still shines And hearts are still ro - manc - ing. Some -

p

C6 Cmi.6 D7 G G C#dim.7

where the band is play - ing And peo - ple still are danc - ing. ———

Am7
D7
G
F9
I know the moon still shines, But things that once were clear,
mf
B♭
Em7
Cm6
D7
Now I scarce - ly see or hear.
Refrain (Slowly, with express.on)
A9
D7
Gmaj.7
G6
G
Gm7
C9
Some-where there's mu - sic, How faint the tune!
p - mf
C7
G9
C7(♭9)
Fmaj.7
F6
F
Some-where there's heav - en, How high the

Fm7
B♭9
B♭7
A♭
B♭7
E♭
E♭maj.7
moon! There is no moon a - bove When
Cm
D7
Gm
Cm6
love is far a - way too, Till it comes
G
Am
D7
G
Gm
Am7
D7
A9
D7
true That you love me as I love you. Some-where there's
mf
p
Gmaj.7
G6
G
Gm7
C9
C7
G9
C7(♭9)
mu - sic, It's where you are, Some-where there's

Fmaj.7
F6
F
Fm7
B♭9
B♭7
A♭
B♭7
heav - en, How near, how far! The dark - est
E♭
E♭maj.7
Cm
D7
G7
night would shine If you would come to me soon,
cresc.
C
Cm
G
Gm
Am7
D7
A9
D7♭9
Un - til you will, How still my heart, How high the
mf
p
1.G
D9+
G6
A9
D7
A9
D7
2. G
C6
Cm6
D7(G)
G6
moon! Some - where there's moon!
mf
mf

FOOLS RUSH IN
(Where Angels Fear To Tread)

Lyrics by
JOHNNY MERCER

Music by
RUBE BLOOM

Dm7
G7
C
Am7
Chorus, Slowly (with expression)
Fools rush in where an-gels fear to tread, and so I come to
mp mf
Dm7
G7
C
you, my love, my heart a - bove my head. Though I
F
G7
C
Am7
see the dan - ger there, if there's a
D7-5
Am7
D7
Dm7
G
Dm7
(G Bass)
chance for me then I don't care. Fools rush in
f
3

G7
C
Am7
Dm7
where wise men nev-er go, but wise men nev - er fall in love
G7
Bb7-5
A7
Dm
so how are they to know? When we met
Fm6
C
Am
Dm
I felt my life be-gin; so o-pen up your heart, and let
ff
G7
1.
C
Fm6
Ab
Dm7
2.
C
Fm6
Ab7
C
this fool rush in. in.

BIG NOISE FROM WINNETKA

Words by
GIL RODIN and
BOB CROSBY

Music by
BOB HAGGART and
RAY BAUDUC

Fm6
Big Noise blew right out a - gain.
C7-9
Fm6
C7-9
Girls were sigh - ing, their boy friends
Fm6
C7-9
Fm6
C7
cry - ing, their hearts were break - ing when
D♭7
C7
Fm6
Big Noise blew in from Win - net

Fm6
ka,
Big Noise
blew right out
a - gain.
Fm6
C7-9
Fm6
Stop,
look,
lis-ten,
Bbm6
C7
Bbm6
C7
lis-ten to the Big Noise.
Fm6
I'm called the Big Noise from Win-net - ka;
mf

Fm6
and I play ro - man - tic parts.
Bbm6
C7+
C7
Fm6
I just blew in from Win-net - ka where I
broke a mil - lion hearts.
Bbm6
C7
Fm
Fm6
C7-9
Now I've had

Fm6
C7-9
Fm6
C7-9
my fun and yet, there's just one who got me
Fm6
C7
Db7
C7
Fm6
from the start. Ex - it
Big Noise from Win-net - ka,
Fm6
en - ter Big Noise in your heart.
ff

IT NEVER ENTERED MY MIND

Words by
LORENZ HART

Music by
RICHARD RODGERS

A7
D7
G7
walk in a daze now, I never go to shows at night, But just to ma-tin-ees now.
Csus4
C
Cm6
poco rit
C9 7
I see the show and home I go.
poco rit
REFRAIN
F
Am
Slowly, with warm expression
p-mf a tempo
Once I laughed when I heard you say-ing That I'd be play-ing
p-mf a tempo
sol-i-taire,
Un-eas-y in my eas-y chair.

B♭6
Gm
E♭7
C7
p
F
Am
It nev - er en-tered my mind. —
Once you told me
mf
p
I was mis-tak - en
That I'd a - wak - en
with the sun —
And or - der or - ange
juice for one, —
It nev - er en-tered my mind.
Em
mp
F6
B♭
Fmaj7
— You have what — I lack my - self, —

B♭6 C7 F6 C7 F B♮dim7 C7 B♭ Am
mf
And now I e - ven have to scratch my back my - self.
mf marcato
B♭ Am C7 F Am F Am F Am
p
Once you warned me That if you scorned me, I'd sing the maid - en's
p
F Am F Am Cm6 B♭+ D7 Gm C7 sus C7
pray'r a - gain. And wish that you were there a - gain To get in - to my
F Fmaj7 B♭6 F C7 1. F6 G7 C7 2. F6
hair a - gain, It nev - er en - tered my mind.
mf
p
Ped. *

PENNSYLVANIA 6-5000

Lyric by
CARL SIGMAN

Music by
JERRY GRAY

Chorus, *Moderately* (*with a swing*)

G C9 G

Num-bers I've got by the doz - en ev - 'ry - one's un - cle and

p - mf

Ddim Am7 D7

cous - in But I can't live with - out buzz - in'

G D7+ G C9

Guitar Tacet (*spoken*)

Penn - syl - van - ia Six, Five Thou - sand I've got a sweet - y I know there

G Ddim Am7

Some - one who sets me a - glow there Gives me the sweet - est "hel -

D7 G Am B7+ B7

Guitar Tacet (*spoken*)

lo there" Penn - syl - van - ia Six, Five Thou - sand We don't say "how are

Em Am B7+ B7 Em E7-5
— you" and ver - y sel - dom ask — "what's new?" — In-
A7 add6 A7 D C7 B7 E9 A7
stead we start and end each call — with "ba - by con - fi - den - tial - ly I —
D7 E♭9 D7 G C9
— love you" — may - be it sounds a bit fun - ny —
G Ddim Am7 D7
When I'm a - way from my hon - ey — here's what I do with my mon - ey —
1. G D+ 2. G G6
Guitar Tacet
(spoken)
Penn-syl-van-ia Six, Five Thou-sand
Penn-syl-van-ia Six, Five Thou-sand

FIVE GUYS NAMED MOE

Words and Music by
LARRY WYNN and JERRY BRESLER

F6
D7
four eyed
Moe,
(fill)
F6
D7
no Moe,
(fill)
Dm6
G9
look at bro - ther,
look at bro - ther,
Gm9
C7
look at bro - ther eat Moe,

Moe.
Moe.
Moe.
Moe.
Moe.
F
F♯°
Gm7
G♯°
Am7
A♭°
Gm7
Gm7/C
Who's the great - est band a - round, makes the cats jump up and down,
F
F7/A
B♭
B°
B♭/C
who's the talk of rhy-thm town, five guys named Moe, that's us.
F
F♯°
Gm7
G♯°
Am7
A♭°
Gm7
C7
When they start to beat it out, ev - 'ry - bo - dy jumps and shouts,

F
F7/A
B♭
B°
B♭/C
F
tell me who the cri - tics all rave a - bout
five guys named Moe, Ah!
F7
We came out of no - where
that don't mean a thing.
G7
N.C./C
to Coda
Fm/C
We rate high
and you'll know why
when you hear us sing,
E♭/C
Fm/C
Cm
sing, sing, sing, sing.

F
F♯°
Gm7
G♯°
F/A
A♭°
Gm7
C7
High brow, low brow, they all a - gree
we're the best in har - mo - ny
I'm
F
F7/A
B♭
B°
B♭/C
D.𝄋 al Coda
tell-ing you folks, you real-ly ought to see five guys named Moe.
CODA
C♭/D♭
sing.

Gb
G°
Abm7
A°
Bbm7
A°
Abm7
Db7
We're the great - est band a - round,— makes the cats jump up and down,
Gb
Gb7/Bb
Cb
C°
Db
we're the talk of rhy-thm town,— five guys named Moe. Not
Ab9
one guy,— (No Moe) not
A9
two guys,— (Little Biddy Moe) not
(ad lib. fill)

B♭9
three guys, (Four Eyed Moe) not
(fill)
C♭9
C9
four guys, (Big Moe) but five guys,
(fill)
Cm9
F6/7
(Eat Moe) five lit - tle guys named
(fill)
B♭6/9
B♭
Moe,
Moe,
Moe,
Moe,
Moe,
that's us.

BEWITCHED

Words by
LORENZ HART

Music by
RICHARD RODGERS

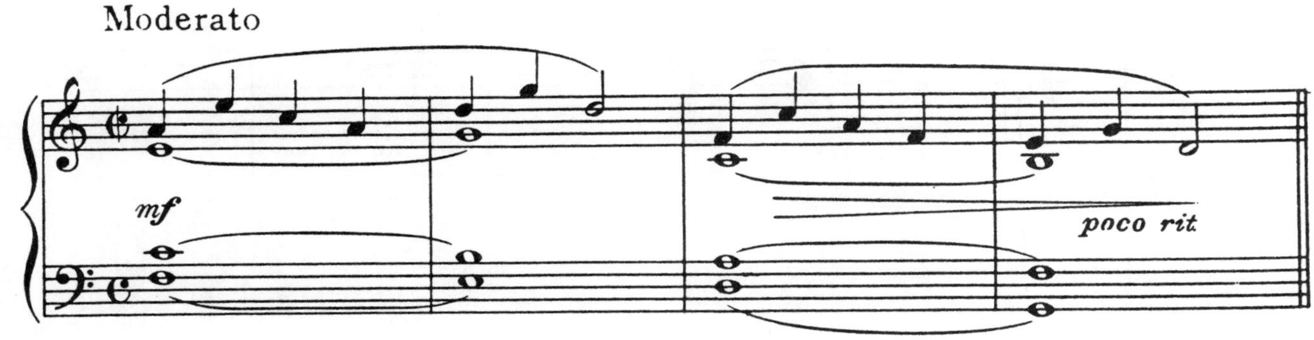

Dm7 G7 C Dm7 G7 C A7
Love's the same old sad sen - sa - tion, Late - ly I've not slept a wink,
Dm7 G7 C Dm7 G7
Since this half-pint im - i - ta - tion, Put me on the blink.
rall.
Refrain (slowly)
C G7 C C+
I'm wild a - gain, Be - guiled a - gain, A sim - per - ing, whim - per - ing
p
F G♯dim C D7 G7 A7
child a - gain, Be - witched, both - ered and be - wild - ered am

Dm
G7
C
G7
I.
Could - n't sleep, And would - n't sleep, When
C
C+
F
G♯dim
C
D7
love came and told me I should - n't sleep, Be - witched, both - ered and be -
G7
C7
F
A7
wild - ered am I.
A7
Am
Lost my heart, but what of it? He is cold I a -
mp

G7 sus.4
G7
C
F♯dim
gree, He can laugh, but I love it, — Al-though the laugh's on
mf
Dm7
G7
C
G7
C
C+
me. I'll sing to him, Each spring to him, And long for the day when I'll
p
F
G♯dim
C
D7
Dm
G7
cling to him, Be - witched, both - ered and be - wild - ered am
1. C
Am
Dm7
G7
2. C
F
C
I. I'm I.
sf

CHATTANOOGA CHOO-CHOO

Lyric by
MACK GORDON

Music by
HARRY WARREN

Dm7 G7 G9 C
— I've got my fare — and just a tri-fle to spare. —
C7 B♭(Csus) C7 F C7 F Gm7 C7 F C7
— You leave the Penn-syl-va-nia sta-tion 'bout a quar-ter to four, — read — a mag-a-zine and then you're
mf
F F9 B♭ Fdim F D+ D7 G-9
in Bal-ti-more, — Din-ner in the din-er, noth-ing could be fin-er than — to have your ham 'n eggs in
A♭m6 C9 F C7 F Gm7 C7
Car-o-li-na. When — you hear the whis-tle blow-in' eight to the bar — Then —

F
C7
F
F9
B♭
Fdim
F
D+
D7
— you know that Ten-nes-see is not ver - y far, — Shov - el all the coal in, got - ta keep it roll-in'
G-9
C7
F
G7
C
Woo, Woo, Chat - ta-noo - ga there — you are. —
mp
C
Cdim
C6
There's gon-na be a cer-tain par - ty at the sta-tion Sat - in and lace, —
Dm7
G7
G9
C
I used to call fun-ny face. —

Cdim
C6
C7
F
She's gon - na cry until I tell her that I'll nev - er roam,
Ab7
D7-5
C
Am7
D7
Dm7
G-9
C
So Chat - ta-noo - ga Choo-Choo won't you choo-choo me home.
Cm6
C7
(Asus)
Cm6
C7
Am7
Chat - ta-noo - ga Choo-Choo won't
D7-5
Dm7
G-9
C
G7
C
C
(Single note)
you choo - choo me home.
sfz

I DON'T WANT TO SET THE WORLD ON FIRE

Words and Music by
SOL MARCUS, BENNIE BENJAMIN and
EDDIE SEILER

Cm7
F9
B♭maj7
Dm7
G9
world - ly ac - claim,
I just want to be the one you love;
and with your ad - mis - sion that
Ped.
Dm7
G9
Dm
C7
C+
you feel the same
I'll have reached the goal I'm dream-ing of
be - lieve me!
3
3
3
Fmaj9
A♭dim
Gm7
B♭m6
I Don't Want To Set The World On Fire,
I
C9
F6
E♭6
E6
F6/9
just want to start
a flame in your heart.
8va

A STRING OF PEARLS

Lyric by
EDDIE DELANGE

Music by
JERRY GRAY

Ab+ Ab6 Ab7 Abmaj7 Ab Abmaj7 Ab7 Ab6 Ab+
wrapped in dreams and filled with love That old string
I've got some - thing {just / else} for you. It's a string
8va bassa
Ab Bb9 Eb7 Ab Bb7
of pearls a - la Wool - worth.
of kiss - es for ba - by.
loco
Eb Ebmaj7 Eb7 Eb6 Eb+ Eb Eb+ Eb6 Eb7
'Til that hap - py day in Spring when {you / I} buy
I found a love so sub - lime, right in that
Ebmaj7 Eb Ebmaj7 Eb7 Eb6 Eb+ Eb F9 Bb7
the wed-ding ring, Please A String Of Pearls a - la
old five and dime, with A String Of Pearls a - la
ff
1 Eb6 Bb7 2 Eb6 D6 Eb6
Wool - worth. Wool - worth.
Wool - worth. Wool - worth.

LOVER MAN
(Oh, Where Can You Be?)

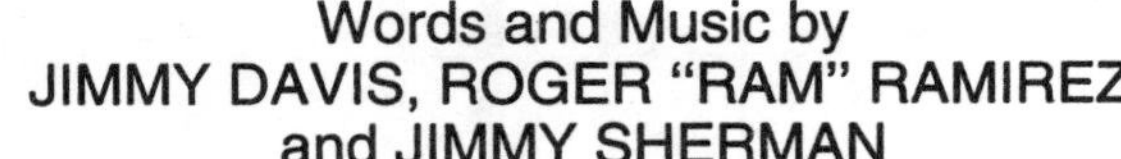

Words and Music by
JIMMY DAVIS, ROGER "RAM" RAMIREZ
and JIMMY SHERMAN

Slow Blues

Em7 Fmaj7 Em7 Fmaj7 E7+9+5

mf

Am7 D7 Am7 D7

I don't know why, but I'm feel - in' so sad,

mf

G9 Dm7/G Dm7 G7 C7+9

I — long to try — some - thing I've nev - er had. — Nev - er had no kiss - in',—

F9
B♭9
G9
C
Em7
E7+5
5 fr.
oh, what I've been miss - in',
lov - er man, oh, where can you be?
Am7
D7
Dm/A
D7
(Inst.)
The night is cold,
and I'm so all a - lone.
Dm7/G
G9
B♭/D
G7
I'd give my soul just to call you my own.
(Inst.)
C7-9
F9
Got a moon a - bove me,
there's no one to love me,
(Inst.)

B♭9
G9
C
Bm7-5
(Inst.) lov - er man, oh, where can you be?
Em
Em+5
Am7
A7
I've heard it said that the thrill of ro - mance can
Dmaj7
A♭7-5
Gmaj7
F♯m7-5
Dm7
Dm+5
be like a heav - en - ly dream. I go to bed
Gm7
3 fr.
G7
Cmaj7
G♭7
Fmaj7
E7+5
5 fr.
with a pray'r that you'll make love to me, strange as it seems.

Am7 D7 Am7 D7 G7 Dm7/G
Some-day we'll meet and you'll dry all my tears and whis-per sweet lit-tle
Dm7 G7 C7+9
things in my ears. Hug-gin' and a kiss-in',
D. S. al Coda
F9 Bb9 G9 C Em7 E7+5
To Coda
ooo, what I've been miss-ing; lov-er man, oh, where can you be?
Coda
Bb9 G9 C7+9
lov-er man, oh, where can you be?
rit.
a tempo
mp

BLUES IN THE NIGHT

Lyrics by
JOHNNY MERCER

Music by
HAROLD ARLEN

Bb
Bb7
F7+5
Bbm7
Eb7
blues in the night, Now the rain's a-fall-in', hear the train a-call-in', whoo-ee, (My
Eb9
Ebm6
F7
ma-ma done tol' me,) Hear dat lone-some whis-tle blow-in' 'cross the tres-tle, whoo-ee, (My
C7
ma-ma done tol' me,) A whoo-ee-duh-whoo-ee, Ol' click-e-ty clack's a-ech-o-in' back th'
blues in the night, The eve-nin' breeze-'ll start the trees to cry-in' and the
broadly

Db7
C+
C7
G+
G7 b5
Bbm6
C7
F7
Ebm6
moon - 'll hide its light, when you get the blues in the night.
R. H.
Abm6
F 7
Eb9
Ebm6
F7
Db7
Take my word, the mock - in' bird -'ll sing the sad - dest kind o'
C+
C7
G+
G-5
Bbm6
C7
F7
Ebm6
song, he knows things are wrong and he's right.
R. H.
Abm6
F7
Bb7
C7
F7
Bb
(whistle)
From Nat-chez to Mo-bile, from

Bb7
Eb7
Mem-phis to St. Joe, where-ev-er the four winds blow; I been in some big towns an'
C7
F7
F+
Bb
F7
heard me some big talk, but there is one thing I know,
A wom-an's a two-face, A
A man is a two-face,
C7
F7
Bb
wor-ri-some thing who'll leave ya t' sing the blues in the night. Hum
Bb7
C7 b9
F7
C7
F7 sus.4
Bb
My ma-ma was right, there's blues in the night.
ppp

LONG AGO
(And Far Away)

Words by
IRA GERSHWIN

Music by
JEROME KERN

F
Dm
Burthen (cantabile)
Gm7
C7
Fmaj.7
Gm
C9
Long a - go and far a - way, I dreamed a dream one
p-mf
F6
C7
F6
D7
Gm7
C7
day And now that dream is here be - side me.
Ab
Bbm7
Eb9
Abmaj.7
G7
Long the skies were o - ver - cast, But now the clouds have
C
C6
Bb
C7
Gm7
C9
F
Dm
passed: You're here at last! Chills run
poco cresc.
p

Gm7 C7 Fmaj7 Gm6 Gm7 C9 F6 C9 C7
up and down my spine, A - lad-din's lamp is mine, The dream I
F6 D7 Gm7 C7 F9 Cm7 F7
dreamed was not de - nied me. Just one look and then I
mf
mf
Bbmaj7 Bb Dm Gm7 F Dm7 Gm7 C7
molto rit.
knew That all I longed for, long a - go, was
molto rit.
1. F Db9 Gb C7(9b) C7
a tempo
you.
2. F
you.
a tempo
dim.
p

THE RIVER SEINE

Original French Text by
FLAVIEN MONOD and GUY LAFARGE
Words by
ALLAN ROBERTS and ALAN BOLT

Music by
GUY LAFARGE

I GOT IT BAD
(And That Ain't Good)

Words and Music by
DUKE ELLINGTON and PAUL WEBSTER

I Got It Bad - 2 - 1

C
Cm6
F#7
G
when the week-end's o - ver and Mon-day rolls a - roun' I end up like I
folks with good in - ten-tions tell me to save my tears I'm glad I'm mad a
mf
Bm7
E7
Ddim
Am
Eb7+5
D7
Edim
G
C
G
start out just cry - in' my heart out He don't love me
bout him I can't live with - out him Lord a - bove me
B7
Em
A7
Em7
A9
A7+5
A7
Am7
like I love him no - bod - y could I Got It
make him love me the way he should I Got It
B7+5
E9
A7
D7-9
1.
G
Em
A9
D7
2.
G
Cm6
G
Bad And That Ain't Good
Bad And That Ain't Good
rall.

THE ANNIVERSARY WALTZ

Words and Music by
AL DUBIN and DAVE FRANKLIN

Moderately

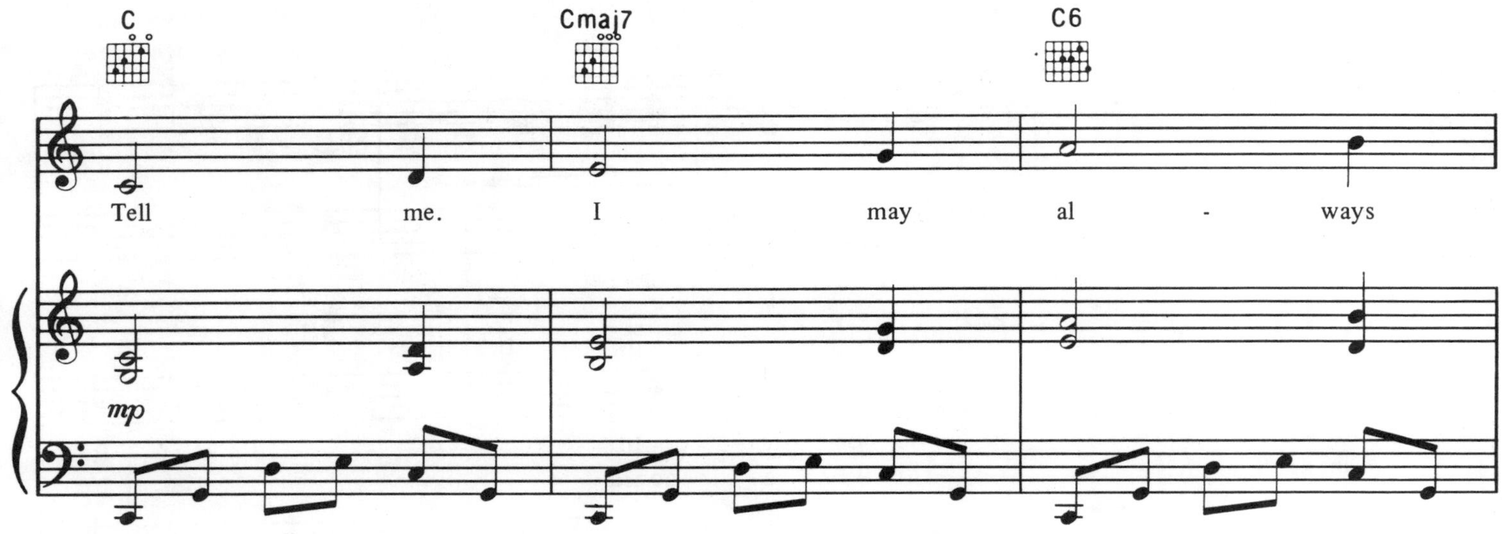

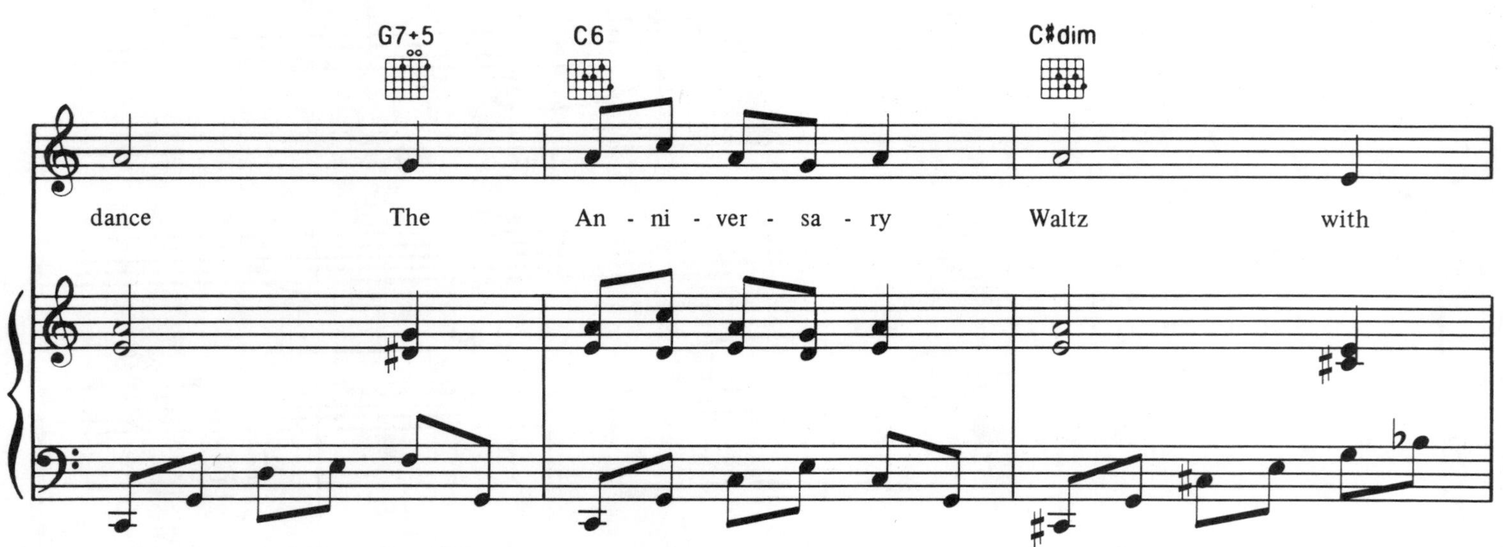

Dm9
G13
Dm
Dm7
you.
Tell me this is
G7
G7
Dm7
real ro - mance, An an - ni - ver - sa - ry
G13
C6
C#dim
Dm7
G13
dream come true.
Let
mf
Gm7
C9
F6
this be the an - them to our fu - ture
ped.

Em7
A7+5
years, To mil - lions of smiles and a
D9
G7+5
C
few lit - tle tears.
8va
May I
loco
mp
ped.
Cmaj7
Em7
A7+5
A7
al - ways lis - ten to The
D9
G7
C
An - ni - ver - sa - ry Waltz with you.
rit.

SKYLARK

Lyrics by
JOHNNY MERCER

Music by
HOAGY CARMICHAEL

Eb
Gm
Ab
Eb
Ab
Eb
green with Spring, Where my heart can go a jour-ney - ing,
F7
Bb7
Eb
Bb7
Eb
O-ver the sha-dows and the rain, to a blos-som cov-ered lane? And in your
Ab
Eb6
Fm7
E7
Eb7
Ab(ma7)
Ebdim
Ab6
Db7
lone-ly flight, Have-n't you heard the mu-sic in the night,
C7
Ddim
C7
Fm
Fm7
Fdim
Db
Fm
Eb7
Ab
Won-der-ful mu-sic, Faint as a 'will o' the wisp," Craz-y as a loon,

G
A7
D7
G
Bb7
Sad as a gyp - sy ser - e - nad - ing the moon. (Oh,)
Eb6
Bb7
Eb
Ab
Eb
Gm
SKY - LARK, I don't know if you can find these things,
Ab
Eb
Ab
Eb
F7
Bb7
But my heart is rid - ing on your wings, So, if you see them an - y
Eb
Bb7
1. Eb
B97
Bb97
2. Eb
E6
Eb6
where, Won't you lead me there? there?

APRIL IN PORTUGAL

English Lyrics by JIMMY KENNEDY
Original Lyrics by LOSE GALHARDO

Music by
RAUL FERRAO

G7
head was in the clouds, My heart went cra - zy
too, And mad - ly I said: "I love
C
you." Too
Cm
soon I heard you
sad re - al - i -
Cm(maj7)
Cm7
Cm6
say: "This dream is for a day," That's
ty, To know it could - n't be, That's

Cm#5
Cm
3fr
G7
Por - tu - gal and love in A - pril! And
Por - tu - gal and love in A - pril! The
G7♭9
4fr
G7
when the show - ers fell, Those tears I know so
mu - sic and the wine con - vinced me you were
G7#5
well, They told me it was spring fool - ing
mine, But it was just the spring fool - ing
C
C
me.
me.
I found my A - pril

G7
dream in Por - tu - gal with you When we dis - cov - ered
C
ro - mance, like I nev - er knew. Then morn - ing brought the
G7
rain, And now my dream is through But still my heart says,
1
C
2
C
"I love you." This you."

LAUGHING ON THE OUTSIDE

Words by
BEN RALEIGH

Music by
BERNIE WAYNE

Cm 3fr. F7 F♯o7 E♭ 3fr. C7+5/-9 C7-9 F7 Fm7 B♭7-9 E♭sus4 B♭sus4
LAUGH-ING ON THE OUT-SIDE, CRY-ING ON THE IN-SIDE 'cause I'm still in love with you.
E♭7 D♭m C+ E♭7 E♭m 6fr. G♭ E♭9 F7
No one knows it's just a pose, pre - tend-ing I'm glad we're a - part. And when I cry my
E♭m B♭+ F7 Cm 3fr. A♭ 4fr. F7/6 F7 B♭7sus4 B♭7 E♭ 3fr. Cm 3fr.
eyes are dry — the tears are in my heart. — My dar - ling, can't we make up?
Fm7 B♭7 Gm7-5 C7+5 C7 Fm G7 Cm 3fr. F7 F♯o7
Ev-er since our break up, make be-lieve is all I do. I'M LAUGH-ING ON THE OUT-SIDE,
E♭ 3fr. C7+5/-9 C7-9 F7 Fm7 B♭7-9 E♭6 F9 B♭7-9 B♭7 E♭6
CRY-ING ON THE IN-SIDE, 'cause I'm still in love with you. The you.
1
2
rall. e dim p

I HAD THE CRAZIEST DREAM

Words by
MACK GORDON

Music by
HARRY WARREN

Moderately

C Gm6 Em7 A7+ Dm Gdim

I had the craz - i - est dream last night, yes I did;

p-mf

Dm Dm7 G7-9

I nev-er dreamt it could be, yet

C Cdim Dm7 G7 Gm6 A7

there you were in love with me. I found your lips close to mine,

Gm6 A7 Dm Gm A7 Dm

so I kissed you, and you did-n't mind it at all.

Am6 B7 Am6 B7 Em E♭dim
When I'm a-wake such a break never-er hap - ens. How long can a {guy / gal} go on dream-
Dm7 G7+ C Gm6 Em7 A7+ Dm C♯dim
ing? If there's a chance that you care, then, please say you do;
Dm Fm6 C E7 Am7 D7 Dm7 G7-9
(Ba-by) say it and make my craz - i - est dream come true.
1. C Dm G7 G7+
2. C A♭7 D♭ C

From the 20th Century-Fox Motion Picture "ORCHESTRA WIVES"

AT LAST

Lyric by
MACK GORDON

Music by
HARRY WARREN

Fmaj7 G7-9 Cmaj7 C6 B Am6 B7-9 Em Am6

dream that I can speak to, A dream that I can call my own, I found a

Cm6 D7 Gmaj7 G6 C Am7 D7-9 G Dm7 G7

thrill to press my cheek to, A thrill I've nev - er known. You

C Am Dm7 G9 Dm7 C Am

smiled and then the spell was cast

Dm7 G7+5 G7 C Am Dm7 G7-9 G7

And here we are in heav - en For you are mine At

1. C Am Dm G7-9 G7

Last. At

2. C6 Fm6 G7-9 C6

Last. *rit.*

Ped. *

JUKE BOX SATURDAY NIGHT

Words by
AL STILLMAN

Music by
PAUL McGRANE

Chorus

F F7
Mop-pin' up so - da pop rick - eys ___ To our heart's de - light

mp_mf

B♭ F Fdim. Gmi.7 Ami. F
Danc-in' to swing - er-oo quick - ies, ___ JUKE BOX SAT-UR-DAY NIGHT. ___

F F7
Good-man and Ky - ser and Mil - ler ___ Help to make things bright,

B♭ F Fdim. Gmi.7 Ami F G♭ F
Mix - in' hot licks ___ with va - nil - la, ___ JUKE BOX SAT-UR-DAY NIGHT.

Cmi.7
F7
Cmi.7
F7
B♭
Faug.
B♭
They put noth - in' past us, — Me and hon - ey lamb, —
Dmi.7
G7
Dmi.7
G7
C7
Gmi.7
C7
Mak - ing one — coke last us — Till it's time to scram; —
F
F7
Mon - ey, we real - ly don't need — that, — We make out — all right,
B♭
F
Fdim.
Gmi.7
Ami.
F
Gmi.7
C7
F
Let-tin' the oth - er guy feed — that — JUKE BOX SATURDAY NIGHT. NIGHT. —

DON'T SIT UNDER THE APPLE TREE
(With Anyone Else But Me)

Words and Music by
CHARLIE TOBIAS, LEW BROWN
and SAM H. STEPT

Don't Sit Under the Apple Tree - 4 - 1

Chorus, Brightly
F
C7
F
D7-9
Don't Sit Un-der The Ap-ple Tree with an-y-one else but me,
mp
Gm7
C7
Gm7
C7
F
Gm7
C7
F
C7
Gm7
C7
An-y-one else but me, An-y-one else but me, No! No! No!
F
C7
F
Cm6
D7
Just re-mem-ber that I've been true to no-bod-y else but you, So
G7
Gm7
C7
F
Bb
F
Gm7
just be true to me.

F
C7
F
D7-9
Don't go walk-ing down lov - ers' lane with an - y - one else but me,
Gm7
C7
Gm7
C7
F
Gm7
C7
F
C7
Gm7
C7
An - y - one else but me, An - y - one else but me, No! No! No!
F
C7
F
Cm6
D7
Don't start show-ing off all your charms in some-bod - y else'- s arms, You
G7
Gm7
C7
F
Gm7
F
F7
Bb
must be true to me. I'm so a - fraid that the
mf

Gm7 C9 F C7 F A7 Dm Dm7
plans we made un-der - neath those moon-lit skies Will fade a - way and you're
Dm6 G9 C7 Dm7 Cdim C7 C7+5 F C7
bound to stray if the stars get in your eyes, So, Don't Sit Un-der The
F F Cm6 D7 G7
Ap-ple Tree with an-y - one else but me, You're my L -
Gm7 C7 1. F Bb F Cdim Gm7 C7 2. F Bb6 F
O - V - E. E.

YOU'D BE SO NICE TO COME HOME TO

From "Something to Shout About"

Words and Music by
COLE PORTER

Bb7 Eb Bb Eb7 Ab
not that you're rar - er Than as - par - a - gus out of sea - son, No, my
B♮ Eb Cm6 Ebdim. Eb Fdim. D7 C
dar - ling, this is the reas - on Why you've got to be mine:
rit p mf
Refrain (rather slow with feeling)
F E7 Am Dm6 E7 Am E7
ten. ten.
You'd be so nice to come home to,
p - mf a tempo
Am C7 F C+
You'd be so nice by the fire,

F
Am
Dm7
B7(♭5)
E7
While the breeze, on high, sang a
D dim.
Am
G7
Am6
F7
B7
lull - a - by, You'd be all that I could de -
mf
E
B7
E
D
E7
Am
Dm6
E7
sire, Un - der stars, chilled by the
p
Am
E7
Am
C7
3
win - ter, Un - der an Aug - ust moon,
cresc.

F C+ F A Dm
Burn - ing a - bove, You'd be
C dim. C F Fm6
so nice, You'd be par - a - dise to come
cresc.
mf espr.
1. C A♭7 D7 G7 C F E7
home to and love. You'd be
f
mf
2. C A♭7 D7 G7 C
home to and love.
f espr.
p

DON'T GET AROUND MUCH ANYMORE

Words by
BOB RUSSELL

Music by
DUKE ELLINGTON

Chorus, Slowly
Guitar Tacit
C
A9
Missed the Sat-ur-day dance Heard they crowd-ed the floor
mf
Am7
D7
G7
C
Could-n't bear it with-out you Don't Get A-round Much An-y-more
Guitar Tacit
C
A9
Thought I'd vis-it the club Got as far as the door
Am7
D7
G7
C
They'd have asked me a-bout you Don't Get A-round Much An-y-more

F
Fm
Em7
C
C7
C7+5
Dar - ling I guess
my mind's more at ease
But
mf
F
Am6
B7
Em
B
G7
Guitar Tacit
C
nev - er-the - less
Why stir up mem-o - ries
Been in-vit - ed on dates
A9
Am7
D7
Might have gone but what for
Aw - f'lly dif-f'rent with - out
you
G7
1. C
Guitar Tacit
2. C
Don't Get A - round Much An - y - more.
Missed the Sat - ur - day
more.
mf
p

SERENADE IN BLUE

Words by
MACK GORDON

Music by
HARRY WARREN

F9
B♭7
B♭7
E♭
B♭7
Fm7
D♭7
like the theme of some for-got-ten mel - o - dy, in the al-bum of my mem-o-ry,
G7
C7
F7
A♭m6
B♭7
E♭
E♭7
A♭6
Ser-e-nade In Blue. It seems like on-ly yes-ter-day, a
p
A♭
E♭m
small ca-fè, a crowd-ed floor and as we dance the night a-way, I
E♭m7
F7
Cm7
hear you say, "For-ev-er more," and then the song be-came a sigh, For-
poco a

Fdim
F7
B♭7
Fm7
ev - er - more be - came good - bye, but you re - mained in my heart.
B♭7
E♭
C7aug
So tell me dar - ling, is there still a spark, or
F9
B♮7
B♭7
E♭
B♮7
Fm7
on - ly lone - ly ash - es of the flame we knew, should I go on whistl - ing in the dark?
G7
G7♭5
C7
F7
E♮7
1 E♭
Fm7
B♭7
2 E♭
B♮7
E♭
Ser - e - nade In Blue. Blue.

I'VE GOT A GAL IN KALAMAZOO

Words by
MACK GORDON

Music by
HARRY WARREN

Eb
Fm7
Eb
Edim
Fm7
Bb7
my, how she grew; I liked her looks, when I car-
Fm7
Bb7
Eb
Eb7
Ab
Eb
ried her books in Kal-a-ma-zoo, zoo, zoo, zoo, zoo. I'm gon-na
G7-9
C7-9
Bbm6
send a wire, hop-pin' on a fly-er, leav-in' to-day.
C7
F7-9
Am I dream-in'; I can hear her scream-in', "Hy-

Bb
Bbdim
Fm7
F9
F7-5
Bb7
Coda
G7
C7
a Mis - ter Jack-son" ev - 'ry-thing's O
hur - ry-ing to.
F9
Bb7
Eb
Eb7
Ab
Abm
Bb7
I'm goin' to Mich - i - gan to see the sweet - est gal in Kal - a - ma -
Eb
Eb7
Ab
Bb7
Eb
Eb7
1.
2.
zoo.
zoo, zoo, zoo, zoo,
Ab
Eb
Ebdim
Bb7
Eb
zoo! Kal - a - ma - zoo!
f

MISTER FIVE BY FIVE

Words and Music by
DON RAYE and GENE DE PAUL

F6
Dm7
Gm7
3 fr
C7
Five by Five he's five feet
tall and he's five feet wide. He don't mea -
- sure no mo' from head to toe than he do
from side to side. Mis - ter
Eb maj7
Emaj7
Fmaj7
N.C.

F6
Dm7
Gm7
C7
Five by Five got fif - teen
F6
Dm7
Gm7
C7
chins and a line of jive. He's a mel -
F6
E♭maj7
Emaj7
Fmaj7
- low ol' cat a real "hep fat" he be Mis -
Gm7
C7
F6
- ter Five by Five.

A7
That man can real - ly jump it for a
D13
fat man. The on - ly trou - ble is there's
G13
no way of know - in' wheth - er he's
Gm7
C7
N.C.
com - in' on or go - in'. Mis - ter

F6 Dm7 Gm7 C7
Five by Five he's slight - ly
F6 Dm7 Gm7 C7
plump on the sol - id side. He don't shake
F6 E♭maj7 Emaj7 Fmaj7
it no mo' from head to toe than he do
Gm7 C7 1 F6 N.C. 2 F6
from side by side. Mis - ter

PISTOL PACKIN' MAMA

IS YOU IS, OR IS YOU AIN'T
(Ma' Baby)

Words and Music by
BILLY AUSTIN and LOUIS JORDAN

Fm/A♭ C7/G Fm N.C. C♭13
still my ba - by, ba - by.
B♭7 E♭7 A♭ Fm7 E♭7♯5 E♭7 A♭ A♭+
Seems my flame in your heart's done gone out. A
D♭ D♭m A♭ A♭7 A♭+
{ wom-an is / man is just } a crea-ture that has al - ways been strange. Just
D♭ D♭m G♭9 F7 B♭m B♭m7/G C7
when you're sure of one you find { she's / he's } gone and made a change.
4fr
3fr

Fm C7/G Fm/A♭ C7/G Fm N.C. C♭13

Is you is, or is you ain't ma' ba - by. __

B♭7 E♭7 G♭9 3 fr F7

May - be ba - by's found some - bod - y new, __ or

B♭7 1 E♭7 A♭ 4 fr Fm7 D♭7 4 fr C7

is ma' ba - by, still ma' ba - by true. __

2 E♭7 A♭ 4 fr N.C.

still ma' ba - by true. __

IT'S MAGIC

(From the Film "ROMANCE ON THE HIGH SEAS")

Words by
SAMMY CAHN

Music by
JULE STYNE

F7 Cm7 F7 F9 Cm7 F7 B♭maj7 B♭ F+ B♭ B°
The stars de-sert the skies and rush to nes-tle in your eyes, IT'S MAG-IC. With-out a gold - en wand or mys-tic
F9 B° F9 Cm G+ Gm7 C7 Gm7 C7-9 Cm7 F9 F7 Cm7 F7-9
3fr.
charms Fan-tas-tic things be-gin when I am in your arms.
B♭ D♭° Cm7 F7 Cm7 F9 B° F7 Cm7 F7
When we walk hand in hand the world be-comes a won-der-land, IT'S MAG-IC. How else can I ex-plain those
F9 Cm7 F7 Fm G7 Fm G7 Fm G7 Cm7 E♭m B♭maj7 Gm7
6fr.
rain-bows when there is no rain, IT'S MAG - IC. Why do I tell my-self These things that hap-pen are all real-ly
C7 B♭ F♯° Gm C7 Cm7 F7-9 B♭ Gm7 Cm7 F7-9 B♭ Gm7 F7-9 B♭
4fr.
1. 2.
true When in my heart I know the mag-ic is my love for you. you.
rall.
pp

PUT 'EM IN A BOX, TIE 'EM WITH A RIBBON
(And Throw 'Em In The Deep Blue Sea)

Words by
SAMMY CAHN

Music by
JULE STYNE

You can take the flow'rs Down in lov-ers' lane and that sen-ti-men-tal po-et-ry, PUT 'EM IN A BOX,
And you won't go wrong If you take a song sung by Frank-ie Boy or Mis-ter C. PUT 'EM IN A BOX,
TIE 'EM WITH A RIB-BON And throw 'em in the deep blue sea. Not for me, All that stuff, The dreams that ruin your sleep,
TIE 'EM WITH A RIB-BON And throw 'em in the deep blue sea. Not for me, All that stuff, The dreams that ruin your sleep,
Not for me, Had e-nough, Love is one thing you can keep. You can take the plans
Not for me, Had e-nough, Love is one thing you can keep. You know what to do
And the wed-ding bells And who-ev-er sings "Oh, Prom-ise Me,"
With old "Tea for Two" And "The Boy for you, The girl for Me,"
PUT 'EM IN A BOX, TIE 'EM WITH A RIB-BON And
throw 'em in the deep blue sea, 'Cause love and I, we don't a-gree.

SINCE I FELL FOR YOU

Words and Music by
BUDDY JOHNSON

Eb
Eb6
Ab6
Bbm7
Ebm
Abm6
Gb
F7
Bb7
Emaj7
Ebm7
Ab7
Ab9
Gm
Cm7
Fm9
F9
Ab
4fr.
6fr.
3fr.
Love bringssuch mis-er-y and pain, I know I'll nev-er be the same
SINCE I FELL FOR YOU.
It's too bad, it's too sad But
I'm in love with you,
You love me then snub me, oh what can I do I'm
still in love with you;
I guess I'll nev-er see the light, I get the blues most ev-'ry
night SINCE I FELL FOR YOU.
YOU.
1.
2.

THEY'RE EITHER TOO YOUNG OR TOO OLD

Words by
FRANK LOESSER

Music by
ARTHUR SCHWARTZ

They're Either Too Young or Too Old - 4 - 1

Brighter tempo
C7
Gm7
C Bass
f
REFRAIN
F
C7
F#dim
Am
Bdim
C9
p-mf
1. They're either too young — or too old, — They're either too gray — or too grassy green, — The pickin's are poor — and the crop is lean, — What's good is in the army, What's left will never harm me. They're either too old —
2. either too warm — or too cold, — They're either too fast — or too fast asleep, — So, darling, believe — me, I'm yours to keep, — There isn't any gravy, The gravy's in the Navy. They're either too fresh.
3. either too bald — or too bold, — I'm down to the wheelchair and bassinet, — My heart just refuses to get upset, — I simply can't compel it to, With no marines to tell it to. I'm either their first.

C7 F Dm6
or too young, So dar - ling, you'll nev - er get stung.
or too stale, There is no a - vail - a - ble male.
breath of spring, Or else I'm their last lit - tle fling.
E7 A E7 A E
To - mor - row I'll go hik - ing with that Ea - gle Scout un - less I
I will con - fess to one ro - mance I'm sure you will al - low, He
I eith - er get a fos - sil or an ad - o - les - cent pup, I
A E7 A E7 A C7 F
get a call from grand - pa for a snap - py game of chess. I'm find - ing it eas -
tries to ser - e - nade me but his voice is chang - ing now. I'm find - ing it eas -
eith - er have to hold him off or have to hold him up. The bat - tle is on,
C7 F Dm6 B♭6 Dm Gm7 C7 1.-2. F G♯dim Gm7 C7
y to stay good as gold.
y to keep things con - trolled. They're eith - er too young or too old. They're
but the fort - ress will hold. They're

3. F
Gm7
C7
Gm7
C7
old. I'll nev - er, nev - er fail ya, while you are in Aus - tra - lia, Or
Gm7
C7
Gm7
C7
Gm7
C7
out in the A - leu - tians, Or off a - mong the Roosh - ians And fly - ing o - ver E - gypt, Your
Gm7
C7
Gm7
C7
Gm7
C7
heart will nev - er be gypped, And when you get to In - di - a, I'll still be what I've been to ya. I've
F
C7
F
rall.
Dm6
B♭6
Dm
Gm7
C7
F
looked the field o - ver, and lo, and be - hold! They're eith - er too young or too old!
rall.

G.I. JIVE

Words and Music by
JOHNNY MERCER

du-ty— is to sa-lute the L - I - E - U - T, — But if you brush the L - I - E - U - T, — The
M. P. makes you K. P. on the Q. T. — This is the G. I. JIVE, man a-live, They
Optional Spoken
give you a pri-vate tank, That fea-tures a lit-tle de-vice called flu-id drive. Jack, af-ter you re-vive, —
Chunk all your junk, Back in the trunk, Fall on your bunk. (Spoken) Clunk! This is the
bunk! (Spoken) Clunk! Soon you're count-in' Jeeps, But be-fore you count to five, —
cresc.
— Seems you're right back digg-in' that G. I. JIVE. —

YOU'LL NEVER KNOW

Words by
MACK GORDON

Music by
HARRY WARREN

Gm
Gm7
C7
F
You'll nev-er know just how much I care.
1. And if I tried, I still could-n't hide my
2. You said good-bye, no stars in the sky re-
Gm
Gm7
C7
Gm
Gm7
C7
love for you. You ought to know, for have-n't I told you
fuse to shine. Take it from me, it's no fun to be a-
F
Db7
Gm
G7
C7
F
Db7
so, a mil - lion or more times? 1. You went a-way and my heart went
lone, with moon-light and mem-'ries. 2.

Gm
Gm7
C7
with you, I speak your name in my ev - 'ry
D7
Am7
Ddim
D7
Ddim
D7
Gm
D
Bbm6
prayer. If there is some oth-er way to prove that I love you, I
F
A7
Cm
D7
Gm
G7
C7
swear I don't know how. You'll nev-er know if you don't know
1.
F
Fdim
Gm7
C7+
2.
F
Db7
F
now. now.

DO NOTHIN' TILL YOU HEAR FROM ME

Words and Music by
DUKE ELLINGTON and
BOB RUSSELL

Cm
G
Am7
D9
G
why peo - ple tear the seam of an - y - one's dream is o - ver my head.
G#dim
Am7
D9
G
Gmaj 7
G7
Do noth - in' till you hear from me At least con - sid - er our ro -
Cmaj7
Cm
G
Am7
D9
G
mance If you should take the word of oth-ers you've heard I have - n't a chance
G
Am7
G
Cm
Eb
Ebmaj7
Eb
Ebmaj7
Cm
True I've been seen with some-one new But does that

Eb Ebmaj7 Eb Eb9 Am7 D7 G E9 Gm
mean that I'm un - true When we're a - part the words in my heart re -
D A7 D7 G Gmaj7/
veal how I feel a - bout you. Some kiss may cloud my mem - o - ry
G7 Cmaj7 Cm G Am7
And oth - er arms may hold a thrill But please do noth - in' till you hear it from me
D9 G
1.
G Bb7 Eb9 D9
And you nev - er will. Do noth - in' till you hear from
2.
G C Cm G

THE TROLLEY SONG

Lyric by
HUGH MARTIN

Music by
RALPH BLANE

2.
Fm7
Bb7
Eb6
mp
He tipped his hat, and took a seat He said he
Fm7
Bb7
Eb6
Am7-5
hoped he had-n't stepped up-on my feet, He asked my name,
D7
Gm7
Bbm
F
Gm7
C7
I held my breath, I could-n't speak be-cause he scared me half to
F7sus4
F7
Fm7
Bb7-9
Eb6
death.
mf
"Buzz, buzz, buzz," went the buzz-er,
Fm7
Bb7
"Plop, plop, plop," went the wheels,

Eb7
Eb9
Eb7
Ab
4 fr.
Abm
4 fr.
Eb6
"Stop, stop, stop," went my heart-strings, As he start-ed to
Bb7-9
Eb
Abm6
Eb6
Gbdim
leave I took hold of his sleeve with my hand, And as
Fm7
Bb9
Edim
Fm7
Bb7
if it were planned He stayed on with me and it was
Eb6
Ab6
G7
Cm
grand, Just to stand with his hand hold-ing mine,
Fm7
Bb9
Eb6
8va
To the end of the line.
f

THE BOY NEXT DOOR

Words and Music by
HUGH MARTIN and RALPH BLANE

Fmaj7
F6
Fmaj7
F6
Gm
Gm7
C7
he does-n't know I ex - ist, No mat - ter how I may per - sist,
she does-n't know I ex - ist, No mat - ter how I may per - sist,
Cm7
F7
F9
F7-9
Bb maj7
Fdim
Bb6
Bb m6
F (addG)
F
So it's clear to see there's no hope for me, Though I live at fif - ty one, thir-ty
So it's clear to see there's no hope for me, Though I live at fif - ty one, thir-ty
five Ken-sing-ton Av - e - nue And he lives at fif - ty one, thir-ty three.
five Ken-sing-ton Av - e - nue And she lives at fif - ty one, thir-ty three.
rit.
CHORUS Slowly
G7-5
G7
F7-5
How can I ig - nore the boy next door? I love him more than I can
How can I ig - nore the girl next door? I love her more than I can
mp

C7
Cm7
F9
Bb
Gm7
Gm6
say. Does-n't try to please me, does-n't e-ven tease me, And he nev-er
say. Does-n't try to please me, does-n't e-ven tease me, And she nev-er
A13-9
A7-9 +5
A7
Dm
Gdim
Cm7
F9
F6
Bbmaj7
Bb6
G7-5
G7
Cm7
F7
F7-5
F7
sees me glance his way. And though I'm heart-sore the boy next door af-
sees me glance her way. And though I'm heart-sore the girl next door af-
Bbmaj7
Bb6
Gm7
C9
C9-5
Bb6
A7
Bb6
A6
Gm7
Cm7
fec-tion for me won't dis-play, I just a-dore him, so I can't ig-
fec-tion for me won't dis-play, I just a-dore her, so I can't ig-
Bm7
Cm7
Bbm7
F9
F6
F7
1.
Bb
Cm7
F7
F6
2.
Bb
Cm7
F7sus4
Bb6
nore him, The Boy Next Door.
nore her, The Girl Next How can Door.
mf
mp
rall.
p

GUESS I'LL HANG MY TEARS OUT TO DRY

Words by
SAMMY CAHN

Music by
JULE STYNE

Slowly, with expression
A6
A+5
A
B
C
B
C
D
E♭
D
E♭
C♯m7
Cm7
har - bor feels.
When I want rain,
Bm7
E7+5
Amaj7
F♯m7
Bm9
E7 6
E7+5
A13
A13-9
I get sun-ny weath-er; I'm just as blue as the sky.
Since love is gone, can't
Dmaj7
G7-5
G7
A/E
B/E
A
C♯m7
F♯9
pull my-self to-geth-er. Guess I'll hang my tears out to dry.
Friends ask me out,
Bm7
E7+5
Amaj7
F♯m7
Bm9
E7 6
E7+5
A13
A13-9
I tell them I'm bus-y, so I must get a new al-i - bi.
I stay at home, and

Dmaj7
G7-5
G7
A/E
B/E
A
ask my-self 'Where is he?' Guess I'll hang my tears out to dry.
G/A
D/A
F/A
C/A
A7-5
Freely
Em7
Dry lit-tle tear-drops,
molto rit.
A7-9
Dmaj7
D6
A9+5
D6
C#7-5
hang-ing on a string of dreams. Fly lit-tle mem-'ries,
F#m7-5
Bm9
F6
E7
Eb9
my lit-tle mem-'ries re-mind him of our cra-zy schemes.

Very broad
Cm7/Ab
Bm7/Ab
Bbm7/Ab
Eb+5/Ab
Abmaj7
Fm7/Ab
Some - bod-y said just for - get a-bout him, so I gave that treat - ment a
Cm7
Eb 7 6
Eb7+5
Ab13
Ab13-9
Dbmaj7
Gb7-5
Gb7
try; Strange - ly e-nough I got a-long with-out him,
Ab
Fm7
Dm9-5
G7-9
Cm7
Cm7/F
F7-9
ten.
then one day he passed me right by, oh well, I
Bbm7
Freely
Ab
G/Ab
Gb/Ab
A/Ab
Eb7
Ab
guess I'll hang my tears out to dry.

SATURDAY NIGHT
(IS THE LONELIEST NIGHT OF THE YEAR)

Words by
SAMMY CAHN

Music by
JULE STYNE

Eb G7 Cm F♯dim Gm A♮dim
Sun-day night at all ’cause thats the night friends come to call And
Bb Gm7 Cm9 F9 Bb7 Fm7 Gm Fm7 Bb7
Mon-day to Fri-day go fast and an-oth er week is past, But
Eb Bb7 Eb Bb7 Eb Bbm C7 E♮dim C+ C7
SAT-UR-DAY NIGHT is the lone- li est night in the week, I sing the
Fm Db7 Fm Db7 Fm Bb7
song that I sang for the mem - ’ries I u - sual-ly seek. Un-til I
Eb G7 Cm Fm7 G7 Cm Abm Eb C7
hear you at the door Un til you’re in my arms once more SAT-UR-DAY NIGHT is the lone-
Fm9 1 Eb Fm7 Eb Fm7 Bb+ 2 Eb Fm7 Eb Ddim Eb
li-est night in the week.
mf

JEEPERS CREEPERS

Words by
JOHNNY MERCER

Music by
HARRY WARREN

Bb
F7
Bb
weath - er vane points, When the weath - er vane points to gloom - y, It's
Dm
A7
Am9
Dm
Bbm6
F
C7
F7
rall.
got - ta be sun - ny to me, When your eyes look in - to mine;
rall.
a tempo
REFRAIN
Dm
F7
(with a swing)
Dm7
Bb6
F7
F9 add Bb
F7
Bb6
Bb
Jeep - ers Creep - ers! Where'd ya get those peep - ers?
mf (with a swing)
Dm
F7
Dm7
Bb6
F7
F9 add Bb
F7
Bb
Jeep - ers Creep - ers! Where'd ya get those eyes?

Dm
F
Dm7
Bb6
F7
F9 add Bb
F7
Bb6
Bb
Gosh all git up! How'd they get so lit up?
Dm
F7
Dm7
Bb6
F7
F9 add Bb
F7
Bb
Gosh all git up! How'd they get that size?
Fm7
Gm
Eb maj. 9
Eb 6
Fm7
Gm
Bb7
Gol - ly gee! When you turn those
Eb maj. 7
Eb
Eb 6
Gm7
Am
F maj. 7
Dm7
heat - ers on, Woe is me!

Gm7
Am
C7
F9 add B♭
F7
Dm
F7
Got to put my cheat - ers on, Jeep - ers
Dm7
B♭6
F7
F9 add B♭
F7
B♭6
B♭
Creep - ers! Where'd ya get those peep - ers?
Dm
F7
Fm6
G7
Cm7
F9 add B♭
F7
B♭
G7
Oh! Those weep - ers! How they hyp - no - tize!
Cm7
F9 add B♭
F7
1 B♭
2 B♭
Where'd ya get those eyes? eyes?

DREAM

Words and Music by
JOHNNY MERCER

Bb F+ Bbmaj7 C7 Co C9 Cm7 3fr. F7 Cm7 3fr.
rise in the air, You'll find your share of mem - o - ries there.
Cm7 3fr. F7-5 Bb A7
So DREAM when the day is thru,
Bb Dm7 G7 Eb
DREAM and they might come true, Things
Ebm Bb A7 D7 Gm7 3fr. Cm7 3fr. F7-9
nev - er are as bad as they seem, So DREAM, DREAM,
1. Bb F13 F7sus4 F7-9 2. Bb F7-9 Bb6add9
DREAM. DREAM.
rall.

'ROUND MIDNIGHT

Words by
BERNIE HANIGHEN

Music by
COOTIE WILLIAMS and THELONIOUS MONK

Ebm Ebm/D Ebm/Db Cm7-5 Fm7-5 Fb9
It be - gins to tell 'round mid - night, 'round mid - night.
Ebm Ebm/D Cm7-5 Bm7(add C#) E7(add C#) Bbm7(add C) Eb7(add C)
7fr 7fr 6fr 6fr
I do pret - ty well till af - ter sun - down.
Abm7 Db9 Fb7 Ebm9 Ab9
4fr 4fr
Sup - per - time, I'm feel - ing sad. But it
3
Cm7-5 F7+5-5 Cb9 Bb9 Fb7-5
4fr 3fr 3fr
real - ly gets bad 'round mid - night.
3

Ebm
Ebm/D
Ebm/Db
Cm7-5
Fm7-5
Fb9
Mem - 'ries al - ways start 'round mid - night, 'round mid - night.
Ebm
Ebm/D
Cm7-5
Bm7(add C#)
E7(add C#)
Bbm7(add C)
Eb7(add C)
Have - n't got the heart to stand those mem - 'ries,
Abm7
Db9
Fb7
Ebm9
Ab9
when my heart is still with you, and old
Cm7-5
F7-5
Cb9
Ab/Bb
Eb(add F)
mid - night knows it too. When some

F7+5
Cb9
Bb9
Fb7-5
Ebm7
quar - rel we had needs mend - ing, does it
Cm7-5
F7+5
Cb9
Bb13
mean that our love is end - ing?
Abm7
Bb7+5
Cm7-5
F7+5
Bb13
Dar - ling, I need you; late - ly I find you're
Eb9+11
Db9+11
Abm7
Fm7-5
Bb7+5
Fb7
out of my arms and I'm out of my mind.

Ebm Ebm/D Ebm/Db Cm7-5 Fm7-5 Fb9
Let our love take wing some mid - night, 'round mid - night.
Ebm Ebm/D Cm7-5 Bm7(add C#) E7(add C#) Bbm7(add C) Eb7(add C)
7fr 7fr 6fr 6fr
Let the an - gels sing for your re - turn - ing.
Abm7 Db9 Fb7 Ebm9 Ab9
4fr 4fr
Let our love be safe and sound when old
Cm7-5 F7-5 Cb9 Ab/Bb Eb(add F)
4fr 4fr 3fr
Tacet
mid - night comes a - round.

Cm7-5
C♭7
Cm7-5
C♭7
F♯m7
B7
Am7
B7
D6/E
7fr
Fm7
B♭13+11
E♭m7
C♯m9
F♯9
3fr
Bm9
E9
Am9
5fr
B♭7-5
E♭6/9
5fr
rit.

RUM AND COCA-COLA

Lyric by
MOREY AMSTERDAM
Additional Lyrics by
AL STILLMAN

Music by
JERI SULLAVAN and PAUL BARON

Chorus, Moderately
C
Dm7
G7
Dm7
G7
Drink-in' Rum And Co-ca Co-la, Go down "Point Koo - mah-nah" Both moth-er and
D9
G7
C
1
F
C
daugh-ter Sing-in' for the Yan-kee dol - lar. An - y
2
F
C
Drink-in' Rum And Co-ca Co-la,
G7
C
Rum And Co-ca Co-la.
mf

ARTISTRY IN RHYTHM

By
STAN KENTON

f
3
f
basso sempre staccato
Ped.
*

ff
3
8va
mf

accel.
f
f
morendo
pp
Ped.
*

MY FOOLISH HEART

Words by
NED WASHINGTON

Music by
VICTOR YOUNG

Bb Gm Cm7 Adim Bbmaj7
lips are much too close to mine, Be - ware My Fool-ish Heart But should our ea-ger
Gm Cm7 D7+5 D7 D7-5 D7 Gm Gm7
lips com-bine Then let the fire start For this time it is - n't fas - ci -
Gb9 Gb7 Bb Dm7-5 G7 Cm7
na - tion, or a dream that will fade and fall a - part, It's love this time, it's
F9 Cm7 F7-9 Bb Gm7 Cm7 F7 Bb Gm7 Cm7 Cb7 Bb6
love, My Fool - ish Heart. The heart.
mp
rall.

From the Broadway Musical Production "BRIGADOON"

ALMOST LIKE BEING IN LOVE

Lyrics by
ALAN JAY LERNER

Music by
FREDERICK LOEWE

Almost Like Being in Love - 2 - 1

F7
F
F+
B♭
Cm7
E♭
F7
B♭
face for the whole hu-man race. Why, it's al-most like be-ing in love!
Am7 D rit.
Bdim.
Am7
D+
G
E♭
All the mu - sic of life seems to be,
Like a bell that is
Am7-5♭
D7
B♭+
D7
Bdim.
E♭
F7
F
F+
ring-ing for me.
And from the way that I feel when that bell starts to
f
ff
B♭
Cm7
E♭7
B♭
Gm
G♭7
B♭
Gm6♮
peal I would swear I was fall - ing, I could swear I was fall - ing, It's al - most like
Gm
D5♭
F7
1 B♭
Fm7
Fm6
Fm7
B♭7
2 B♭
be - ing in love.
What a love.
L.H.
f
ff
rit.
8

GIVE ME THE SIMPLE LIFE

From "WAKE UP AND DREAM"

Words by
HARRY RUBY

Music by
RUBE BLOOM

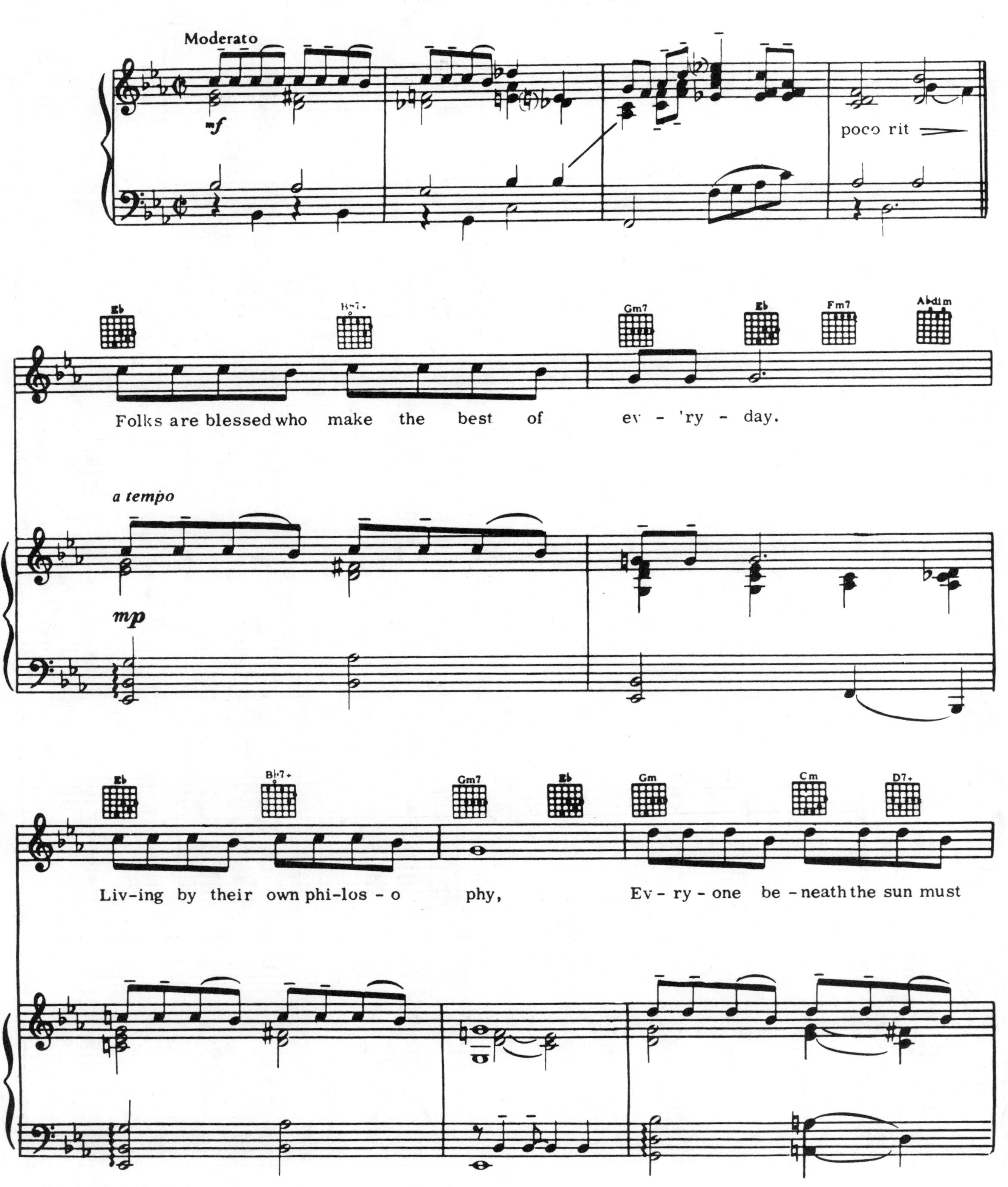

Gm
Fm
Ab+
Fm7
Fm7
Abm
Bb7
find a way, — and I have found the on - ly way for me.
rit.
Fm7
Bb7
Ebmaj7
C7
Fm
Refrain Rhythmically, but not fast
I don't be - lieve in fret - tin' and griev - in'; why —
Liv - ing I find is best — when your mind is keen —
mp-f
a tempo
G7
Cm
G7
Eb7
Cm
Abm
Eb
— mess a - round with strife; — I nev - er was cut out to —
— as a carv - ing knife. — I'm cra - zy a - bout sleep, can't —
Cm
Fm7
C9
F7
F7+
Bb9
Fm7
— step and strut out. Give — me the sim - ple life! — Some —
— do with - out sleep. Give — me the sim - ple life! — I —

Bb7 Ebmaj7 C7 Fm G7 Cm
find it pleas-ant din - ing on pheas-ant. Those things roll off my knife;
love to whit-tle and play a lit-tle tune on a ten-cent fife;
G7 Eb7 Cm Abm Eb Cm Fm7
just serve me to-ma-toes and mashed po-ta-toes; give
I don't aim to wor-ry, hus - tle or hur-ry; give
Bb7 Eb Fm7 Bb9
me the sim-ple life. A cot-tage small is all I'm
me the sim-ple life. I greet the dawn when I a-
Eb Fm7 Bb9 Eb
af - ter, not one that's spa-cious and wide. A
wak - en, the sky is clear up a - bove. I

Fm G7-9 Cm Cm7 F9
house that rings with joy and laugh-ter and the ones you love in -
like my scram-bled eggs and ba - con served by some - one that I
Fm7 Bb7 Fm7 Bb7 Ebmaj7 C7 Fm
side. Some like the high road, I like the low road, free-
love. Life could be thrill - ing with one who's will - ing to
G7 Cm Eb7 Cm Abm Eb
from the care and strife. Sounds corn - y and seed - y, but
be a farm-er's wife; kids call - ing me pap - py would
Cm Fm7 Bb7 Eb Ebdim
1.
2.
yes, in-deed-y; give me the sim-ple life!
make me hap-py; give me the sim-ple life!
fz

ON THE ATCHISON, TOPEKA AND THE SANTA FE

Lyric by
JOHNNY MERCER

Music by
HARRY WARREN

Ebmaj7
Ab6
Ab
4 fr.
Ebmaj7
Ab6
Eb
Ab6
Hey, Jim! yuh bet-ter git the rig!
Ooh,
Ooh,
Ooh,
Ebmaj7
Ab6
Cm
Ebmaj7
Fm6
Cm7
She's got a list o' pas-sen-gers that's
Fm7
Dm7-5
G7
C
pret-ty big. And they'll all want lifts to
Brown's Ho - tel, Cause
F
C
G+
C
Cmaj7
lots o' them been trav-el-in' for quite a spell, All the way from Phil-a-
C7
F6
D7-5
C
G♯dim
Am
Dm7
G7
C
del-phi - ay, On The Atch-i-son, To-pe-ka And The San-ta Fe.

HEY! BA-BA-RE-BOP

Words and Music by
LIONEL HAMPTON and CURLEY HAMMER

D7♯5
G6
Am7
G6/B
Am7
A♭7
4fr
yes, your ba - by knows. Ma -
G6
F9
D7
G6
til - da Brown told Old King Tut, if you can't say re - bop, keep your
G7
C9
big mouth shut, sing - in': Hey! Ba - ba - re - bop. Hey!
G6
Am7
G6/B
B♭dim7
Am7
D7
D7♯5
Ba-ba-re-bop. Hey! Ba-ba-re-bop, yes,

G6
Am7
G6/B
Am7
A♭7
4fr
G6
your ba - by knows.
Ma-ma's on the chair,
F9
G6
D♭9
Pa-pa's on the cot,
ba-by's in the crib blow-in' his nat-'ral top,
sing-in': Hey!
C9
G6
Am7
G6/B
B♭dim7
Ba-ba-re-bop.
Hey!
Ba-ba-re-bop.
Hey!
Am7
D7
D7♯5
G6
Am7
Ba - ba - re - bop,
yes,
your ba - by knows.

G6
F9
Up on the moun-tain,
look-in' at the sea,
G6
G7
C9
look-in' for that cat that stole my
ba-by from me,
sing-in': Hey! Ba-ba-re-bop.
G6
B♭dim7
Am7♭5
Cm6
G♯dim7
Hey! Ba-ba-re-bop.
Hey! Ba-ba-re-bop,
Cm6
G6
G6/F
C/E
Cm6/E♭
G6/D
3 fr
G6
yes,
your ba - by knows.

From the Twentieth Century-Fox Technicolor Musical "BILLY ROSE'S DIAMOND HORSESHOE"

THE MORE I SEE YOU

Words by
MACK GORDON

Music by
HARRY WARREN

Refrain, with feeling
Fm7
Ebdim
Eb
Bb7
Ebmaj7
The more I see you, the more I want you. Some-how this
feel - ing just grows and grows. With ev - 'ry
Ebm
Dbm
Gb7
Cb
Abm7
sigh I be - come more mad a - bout you; more lost with-
F9
out you, and so it goes. Can you im -

Eb
Bb7
Eb
Ebmaj7
Fm7
Bb7
Fm7
Ebdim
ag - ine how much I'll love you, the more I
Eb
Bb7
Eb
Bb+
Bbm7
Eb7
Bbm7
Eb7
Dbm
Bbdim
Ab
see you as years go by? I know the on - ly one for
Abm
Eb
C7
F7
Eb
Fm7
Fdim
me can on - ly be you. My arms won't free you, my heart won't
1.
Eb
Fm7
Ebdim
2.
Eb
Ab9
Eb
try. The more I try.

I CAN'T BEGIN TO TELL YOU

Words by
MACK GORDON

Music by
JAMES V. MONACO

Broadly
C Cmaj7 Gm6 A7 A+ Am7 Dm A7 Dm D9
I can't be - gin to tell you, how much you mean to me. My
pmf
G7 F6 F+ G7 C Edim Dm F G7 C Cmaj7
world will end if ev-er we were through. I can't be - gin to
Gm6 A7 Dm A7 Dm Am Dm D7 D9 G7 Em
tell you how hap-py I would be, if I could speak my
G9 Em G7 C Ab7 Fm C Dm6
mind like oth - ers do. I make such pret - ty

E7
A7
G6
Cdim
A7
A9
Bm
Bbm
D9
speech-es, when - ev - er we're a - part. But, when you're near, the
Bm
Ebm6
D+
Dm
G7
G9
F
Gdim
G7
C
Cmaj7
words I choose re - fuse to leave my heart. So, take the sweet - est
Gm6
A7
A+
Am7
Dm
A7
Dm
Dm6
Cdim
C
Cdim
phras-es the world has ev - er known, and make be - lieve I've
Dm7
Em
G7
1. C
Em7
Am
Cm7
Dm
F
G7
2. C
Am6
Fm
C
said them all to you. I you.

LAURA

Lyric by
JOHNNY MERCER

Music by
DAVID RAKSIN

Slowly with expression
Chorus
Am7
D7-9
G
Lau - ra is the face in the mist - y light
mp
Gm7
C7-9
Fmaj7
F6
Foot - steps that you hear down the hall
Fm7
Abm6
Bb7-9
Ebmaj7
Eb
The laugh that floats on a sum - mer night That you can
Cm6
D7-9 -5
4 fr.
D9-5
4 fr.
D7
Bm
G
E9
E7-9
Am7
nev - er quite re - call And you see Lau - ra

D7-9
G
Gm7
on the train that is pass - ing thru
Those eyes
C7-9
Fmaj7
F6
Fm7
how fa-mil - iar they seem
She gave
Fdim
C
D7
D7-9 -5 4 fr.
D7-9 +5 4 fr.
your ver - y first kiss to you
That was Lau - ra
G9
G7-9
1. C
E9
E7-9
2. C
but she's on - ly a dream.
dream.
rall.
p

I'M BEGINNING TO SEE THE LIGHT

Words and Music by
DUKE ELLINGTON, HARRY JAMES,
JOHNNY HODGES and DON GEORGE

I'm Beginning to See the Light - 3 - 1

G6
Eb7
D7
G6
Eb7
D7
never went in for after - glow __ or can - dle - light on the
Eb7
G6
Em
D7
G
Dm6/F
E7
mis - tle - toe, __ but now when you turn the lamp down low, __ I'm be -
A7
Am7
D7
G
B7
gin - ning to see the light. __ Used to ram - ble
Bb7
through the park, __ shad - ow - box - ing in the dark. __

A7
Eb7
Then you came and caused a spark _ that's a four a - larm fire ___ now. _
Am7
D7
G6
Eb7
D7
G6
___ I nev - er made love by lan - tern shine, _ I
Eb7
D7
Eb7
G6
Em
D7
nev - er saw rain - bows in my wine, _ but now that your lips are
G Dm6/F E7
A7
Am7
D7
1 G Gm7b5 D9
5 fr
4 fr
2 G D7#5(b9) G6
4 fr
burn - ing mine, _ I'm be - gin - ning to see the light. _ I ___
8vb

OLD DEVIL MOON

Words by
E. Y. HARBURG

Music by
BURTON LANE

Old Devil Moon - 3 - 1

Abm7
Db7
Gb
C7
F
C7
F
Eb/F
old dev-il moon in your eyes.
You and your glance
mf
mp
3
F
Eb/F
D
Dmaj7
D
Dm
make this ro-mance too hot to han-dle.
Stars in the night
Dm7
G7
C7
Bb/D
Ebm
blaz-ing their light can't hold a can-dle to your raz-zle daz-zle.
F
Eb/F
F
Eb/F
F
You've got me fly-in' high and wide on a mag-ic car-pet ride

Eb/F
F
C7(b5)
F9
F7(b9)
Bbmaj9
Bb
full of but-ter-flies in - side.
Wan-na cry, wan-na croon, wan-na
Bbm7
Abm7
Db7
Gb
C7
F
C7
laugh like a loon. It's that old dev - il moon in your eyes.
mf
F
Cm7
F
Cm7
F
C7
Cm7
F
Cm7
Just when I think I'm free as a dove, old dev-il moon deep in your
mf
1.
F
Eb
C7(b5)
F
C7(b5)
2.
F
Cm7
F
eyes blinds me with love.
eyes blinds me with love.
f
f l.h.

A SUNDAY KIND OF LOVE

Words and Music by
BARBARA BELLE, LOUIS PRIMA,
ANITA LEONARD and STAN RHODES

F6
Am7
A♭m7
Gm7
C7♭9
Am7
D7♭9
love that's on the square._
Can't seem to find some - bod - y to care._
Gm7
B♭m6
Am7
D7
Gm7
C7+5
Gm7/C bass
I'm on a lone - ly road that leads me no - where._
I need a Sun - day kind of
F6
Cm7
F9
love.
I do my Sun - day dream - ing and
Cm7
F7♭9
B♭6
Cm7
F7♭9
B♭6
all my Sun - day schem - ing ev - 'ry min - ute, ev - 'ry hour,_ ev - 'ry day.
I'm

G9
Dm7
G9
Dm7
G7♭9
C9
F♯dim
hop - ing to dis - cov - er a cer - tain kind of lov - er, who will show me the way.
Gm7
Tacet
F6
Am7
A♭m7
Gm7
C7♭9
Am7
D7♭9
My arms need some - one to en - fold, to keep me warm when Mon - days are cold,
Gm7
B♭m6
Am7
D7
Gm7
C7+5
Gm7/C bass
a love for all my life to have and to hold. I want a Sun - day kind of
1. F6
D7♭9
Gm7
Tacet
2. F6
Gm7
B♭m6
Fmaj7
love. I want a love.
rit.

COME RAIN OR COME SHINE

Words by
JOHNNY MERCER

Music by
HAROLD ARLEN

C7
ten.
F7
deep as a riv - er, Come rain or come shine.
ten.
Gb Cm7 F7
Bbm
Fm
I guess when you met me It was
molto espr.
Bbm
C7(b5)
Fm
just one of those things, But don't ev - er
Ebm
Adim Fdim C7 Bbdim
Cdim G7 G7(b5) C9
bet me, 'Cause I'm gon - na be true if you let me.
mf dim
rit

F
a tempo
A7
You're gon - na love me Like no - bod - y's loved me, Come
p a tempo
Dm
Dm
rain or come shine.
Hap - py to - geth - er, Un -
B9
B7
A7
hap - py to - geth - er And won't it be fine.
D7
Days may be cloud - y . Or
poco f

G7
rit
Gm
sun - ny, We're in or we're out of the mon - ey, But
rit
Dm7
a tempo
G7
G
E7(♭5)
A
I'm with you al - ways, (Au - gie,) (Del - la,)
I'm with you rain or
a tempo
f
1. D7
G7
E♭maj.7 E♭7
2. D7
shine!
shine!
rit e dim
p dim e rall.
G7
C7
D
pp

From the Motion Picture "THE TIME, THE PLACE & THE GIRL"

A GAL IN CALICO

Words by
LEO ROBIN

Music by
ARTHUR SCHWARTZ

E♭ E♭maj7 E♭6 E♭maj7 Fm7 B♭9 B♭7(♭9)
Work - in' with a ro - de - o, go from town to town.
Gon - na quit the ro - de - o, gon - na set - tle down,
E♭ E♭maj7 E♭6 E♭maj7 Fm7 B♭9
See most ev - 'ry kind - a gal, ev - 'ry kind - a gown. But
buy a bolt of cal - i - co for a wed - din' gown. Then,
E♭ B♭m7 E♭7 A♭maj7 Fm7 G7 C7 F9(♭5) B♭7
who made my heart sing?
will I fence her in.
Yip - pee yi! Yip - pee yo! My
E♭ Cm7 Fm7 B♭9 E♭ Fm7 B♭7 E♭
lit - tle gal in cal - i - co.
pp

FIVE MINUTES MORE

Words by
SAMMY CAHN

Music by
JULE STYNE

G7 Dm7 G6 7 G7 C E7+5 E7
— let me stay — in your arms. — Here am I beg-ging for On-ly
p mf
F A7+5 A7 Dm D7 G7 Dm7 G7 C Dm7 C C7+5
FIVE MIN-UTES MORE, On-ly FIVE — MIN-UTES MORE — of your charms. —
F Fm C Co7 C G7 C7-9 F C E7 Am
All week long I dreamed a-bout our Sat-ur-day date. — Don't you know that Sun-day morn-ing
f
D7 G7 C E7+5 E7 F A7+5 A7 Dm D7
you can sleep late? — Give me FIVE MIN-UTES MORE, On-ly FIVE MIN-UTES MORE, Let me stay,
p mf
G7 Dm7 G7 1C Dm7 Am7 Ebo7 G7 2C Dm7 Ab7 Dm7 G9 C6
— let me stay — in your arms. — Give me. —
f p f

YOU MAKE ME FEEL SO YOUNG

Words by
MACK GORDON

Music by
JOSEF MYROW

B♭ B♭m B♭dim Gm7 C9 F7
do the cause of it all is you.
B♭ Fdim Cm7 F7 B♭ Fdim
You make me feel so young, You make me feel so
p-mf
Fm7 F7 B♭ B♭7 B♭7+ E♭maj7 Cm7
spring has sprung, And ev - 'ry time I see you grin, I'm such
Dm7 Gm7 C7 F7 B♭ Fdim
a hap - py in - di - vid - u - al. The mo - ment that you speak,

Cm7 F7 B♭ Fdim Fm7 F7
I wan-na go play hide and seek,
B♭ B♭7 B♭7+ E♭maj7 Cm7 Dm7 Gm7 C7 F7
I wan-na go and bounce the moon, just like a toy bal-loon.
B♭7 B♭dim B♭7 E♭dim
You and I are
B♭7 Fm7 B♭7 E♭dim
just like a coup-le of tots,
run-ning a-cross a
3
3

Gm7
B♭dim
E♭
Cm
G7
Cm
C7
F7
Cm7
F7
C♭
B♭
mead-ow, pick - ing up lots of for - get - me - nots.
Fdim
Cm7
F7
B♭
Fdim
You make me feel so young.
You make me feel there are
Fm7
F7
B♭
B♭+
E♭maj7
E♭m
songs to be sung, bells to be rung, and a won - der - ful fling to be
B♭
Dm6
Fdim
Cm7
F7
B♭
Dm6
Fdim
flung.
And e - ven when I'm old and gray,

Cm7
F7
D7+
D7
G7-9
I'm gon-na feel the way I do to - day, 'cause
Cm
G7
Cm
C7
F7
Bb
Gm7
Cm7
F7
F7+
1.
You make me feel so young.
ff
Bb
Gm7
Cm7
F7
F7+
Bb
Gm7
2.
young.
Cm7
F7
F7+
Bb

'TIS AUTUMN

Words and Music by
HENRY NEMO

E♭
Gm
C
Fm
A♭m6
Charmed all the way-side, there's no dis-pute, now, shed-ding leaves, they
E♭
F7
Fm7
B♭7
E♭
don't give a hoot, La-de-da-de-da-de-dum 'Tis Au-tumn. Then the
mf
B♭m7
E♭7
B♭m7
E♭7
birds got to-geth-er to chirp a-bout the weath-er
Mmm.........
Whistle-opt.....
A♭6
E♭+
A♭6
Cm7
F7
Aft-er mak-ing their de-cis-ion in

Cm7
F7
Bb7
F7
Bb7
bird-y-like pre-cis-ion, turned a-bout and made a bee-line to the south. My
Fm7
Bb7 +5
D7
Eb
Gm
hold-ing you close real-ly is no crime, ask the birds, the trees and
C7
Fm
Abm6
Eb
F7
Ole Fath-er Time. It's just to help the mer-cu-ry climb
Fm7
Bb7
1. Eb
Bb7
2. Eb6
La-de-da-de-da-de-dum 'Tis Au-tumn. Ole Au-tumn.

WUNDERBAR
(From "KISS ME KATE")

Words and Music by
COLE PORTER

D7
D
Em7
F°
D7
dream— come true.
Refrain
G
Wun - der - bar, wun - der - bar! What a
p-mf
C
G
D7
per - fect night for love, Here am I,
mf
G
here you are, Why, it's tru - ly wun - der -

G
bar! Wun - der - bar, wun - der - bar!
C
G
We're a - lone and hand in glove, Not a
D7
cloud near or far, Why, it's
mf
G
more than wun - der - bar! Oh I

Fm7
Bb7
Eb
care, dear, for you mad - ly, And I
mf
long, dear, For your kiss. I would
Am7
D7
G
C#m7
die, dear, for you glad - ly, You're di - vine, dear!
cresc.
f
rit.
F#7
D9
G
And you're mine, dear! Wun - der - bar, wun - der-
subito p e rall.
mp a tempo

C
G
bar! There's our fav' - rite star a - bove,
D7
What a bright shin - ing star, Like our
rit
1
G
D7
love, it's wun - der - bar! Wun - der -
2
G
love, it's wun - der - bar!
f
p

I'LL NEVER SMILE AGAIN

Words and Music by
RUTH LOWE

*Chord names and diagrams for guitar

Refrain
E♭
E♭dim
Fm7
B7
B♭7
A♭
E♭
I'LL NEV - ER SMILE A - GAIN Un-til I smile at you
a tempo
p - f
Fm7
B7
B♭7
D♭
D
I'll nev - er laugh a - gain What good would it do?
B7+5
A♭m
B♭+5
E♭maj.7
D9
For tears would fill my eyes My heart would re - a - lize, That
G
D7
G
our ro - mance is through I'll nev - er love a-gain

B7
Bb7
Ab
Eb
Ebdim
Fm7
I'm so in love with you. I'll nev - er thrill a - gain
B7
Bb7
Eb7
Cm
Ebdim
Eb7
Abmaj.7
Ab6
to some-bod - y new With - in my
Abm
Eb
Gm7
C7
Fm7
heart I know I will nev - er start to smile a - gain
Fm7
B7+5
Bb7
1. Eb
Ebdim
Bb7
Eb
Ebdim
2. Eb
B7
Eb
Un-til I smile at you. I'LL NEV-ER you.

SO IN LOVE

From "Kiss Me Kate"

Words and Music by
COLE PORTER

Db G7 C C7b9 Fm
love with you am I, Ev - en with-
poco marc.
p
C7 Fm Bbm
out you, My arms fold a - bout you, You
Eb Db Dbm Abmaj7 Ab6 Eb7 Db Eb7
know, dar - ling, why, So in love with you am
mf
Ab Db Eb7 Ab
I, In love with the night mys - te - ri - ous, The
mf più espressivo

Db
Eb7
Ab
Db
Eb7
night when you first were there,
In love with my joy de-
cresc. più espr.
Ab
Abmaj7
Ab6
C7
Fm
Fm7
Dm7-5
G7
C
C7b9
lir - i - ous
When I knew that you could care,
So
poco marc.
Fm
C7
Fm
taunt me
and hurt me,
De - ceive me,
De -
p
Bbm
Eb
Eb7
Cm7-5
F7
sert me.
I'm yours 'til I die,
So in
cresc.
f passionately

Bbm
Dbm
Ab
Abm
Ab°
love, So in love, So - in love with you, my
dim.
Bbm7
Eb7
1.
Ab
C7
love am I.
f
2
Ab
I.
f
poco allarg.
Ped.
p *

CEMENT MIXER
(Put-Ti, Put-Ti)

Words and Music by
SLIM GAILLARD and LEE RICKS

Guitar tacet
F
F7
Fdim
F7
A pud-dle o' veet! con-crete. First you get some gra-vel,
Bb
F7
Bb
F
Em
G7
F
Em
Dm
Pour it in the vout, To mix a mess o' mor-tar you add ce-ment and wa-ter.
C7
Guitar tacet
F6
Fm6
F6
Gm7
C7
See the mel-low roon-y come out, slurp, slurp, slurp. CE-MENT MIX-ER! Put - ti, Put-ti,
F
Fm6
F6
Gm7
C7
F6
Fm6
F7
CE-MENT MIX - ER! Put - ti, Put-ti, CE-MENT MIX - ER! Put-
Bb
Bbm
F
Guitar tacet
1 F
2 F
F6
ti, Put-ti, Who wants a buck-et of ce-ment? ment?
sfz

ALWAYS TRUE TO YOU IN MY FASHION

Words and Music by
COLE PORTER

B13
Cdim7 A/C♯
mf
C C9 E7
dolce rit.
f
Suddenly hot
slave?
I'm just mad for you, And I'll al - ways be, But nat - ur - al - ly
mf
dolce rit.
p
Medium bounce
A6
Dmaj7
A6
If a cus - tom tail - ored vet
Asks me out for some-thing wet,
asked to have a meal
By a big ty - coon in steel,
p
Dm(maj7)
A
A/C♯
Cdim7
E7/B E7
When the vet be - gins to pet,
I cry "hoo - ray!"
If the meal in - cludes a deal,
ac - cept I may!
mf
E♭7/G E7/G♯ E9
A/C♯
A+/C♯
D
G♯/B♯ F♯m/C♯ A/C♯
But I'm al - ways true to you, dar - lin', in my fash - ion,
p
f

Bm7/D
A/E
B9
Dm/E Bm/E
A
D
A/C♯
Yes, I'm al - ways true to you, dar - lin' in my way.
p
Cdim7
Bm7
E
A6
Dmaj7
A6
I en - joy a ten - der pass By the boss of Bos - ton
I could nev - er curl my lip To a dazz - lin' dia - mond
p
Dm(maj7)
A
A/C♯
Cdim7
E7/B
E7
Mass. Though his pass is mid - dle class and not "Black Bay!"
clip, Though the clip meant "let 'er rip" I'd not say "Nay!"
mf
E♭7/G
E7/G♯
E9
A/C♯
A+/C♯
D
G♯/B♯
F♯m/C♯
A/C♯
But I'm al - ways true to you, dar - lin', in my fash - ion,
p
f

Bm7/D A/E B9 Dm/E Bm/E A D A/C#
Yes, I'm al - ways true to you, dar - lin' in my way.
p
Bm7 A D Dmaj7 D6 Dm A Amaj7
There's a mad - man known as "Mack" Who is plan - ning to at -
There's an oil man known as "Tex" Who is keen to give me
A A7 D F#7/C# B9
tack, If his mad at - tack means a Cad - il - lac, O -
checks And his checks I fear, mean that Tex is here to
E D#m7♭5/E E7 A6/E E9 A/C# A+/C# D G#/B#
kay!
stay!
But I'm al - ways true to you, dar - lin', in my
pp dolce

F♯m/C♯ A/C♯
A9
Bm7♭5/D
Bm7♭5
1
A/E
fash - ion,
Yes, I'm al - ways true to you,
f
subito p
B9
Dm/E
E9
A6
Cm7/G
E7/G♯ Bm
E7/G♯
dar - lin', in my way.
I've been
f
ff
2
A/E
B13
Dmaj7/E
Bm7/E
al - ways true to you,
dar - lin', in my
ff
A
D6
N.C.
E7♯5/B♭
A7
way.
3